IMAGES
of America

PANTHER PRIDE
UNIVERSITY OF PITTSBURGH
MEN'S BASKETBALL

The formation of the Eastern Athletic Association (Eastern Eight) in 1976 breathed fire and life into the University of Pittsburgh-Duquesne University basketball rivalry, and, for a period of six or seven years, no sporting event in Pittsburgh produced as much excitement, drama, or hard feelings. Both universities were charter members of the new conference. This meant that the University of Pittsburgh Panthers and the Duquesne University Dukes would play at least two regularly scheduled games each season from 1976 to 1982. Both Pitt and Duquesne thrilled huge crowds at both the Civic Arena and Fitzgerald Field House.

IMAGES
of America

PANTHER PRIDE
UNIVERSITY OF PITTSBURGH
MEN'S BASKETBALL

Sam Sciullo Jr.

ARCADIA
PUBLISHING

Published by Arcadia Publishing
Charleston, South Carolina

Library of Congress Catalog Card Number: 2002106714

For all general information contact Arcadia Publishing at:
Telephone 843-853-2070
Fax 843-853-0044
E-mail sales@arcadiapublishing.com
For customer service and orders:
Toll-Free 1-888-313-2665

Visit us on the Internet at www.arcadiapublishing.com

Acknowledgments

I want to thank some special people for their assistance and contributions during the completion of this project, including Melissa Androutsos, E.J. Borghetti, Brad Cuprik, and Burt Lauten from the University of Pittsburgh Athletics Media Relations Office. My appreciation also goes to John Antonik and Joe Swan from the West Virginia University Sports Communications Office. Joe Onderko from Westminster College was most helpful throughout. My thanks go to Chris Weber for help in finding specific photographs, to Miriam Meislik from University Archives, and to Maria Carpico from the Pittsburgh Post-Gazette. I also want to say thank you to some photographers who have always been ready and willing to go above and beyond the call of duty: Will Babin, Harry Bloomberg, Sean Brady, Mike Drazdzinski, Charles LeClaire, and William McBride.

CONTENTS

College basketball coaches have some of the best seats in the house from which to view the action, but Georgetown University head coach John Thompson had an unexpected seat-crasher at his post when Pitt forward Brian Shorter ended up in Thompson's lap during action from the February 11, 1989 game between Pitt and Georgetown at the Civic Arena in Pittsburgh. The Panthers and the Hoyas played many of their Big East Conference games at the downtown Civic Arena in Pittsburgh. Pitt defeated the Hoyas 79-74 in this contest, avenging an earlier 76-57 loss to Georgetown in Washington, D.C. Georgetown won a third meeting between the schools 85-62 in the Big East Tournament at Madison Square Garden in New York City one month later. (Photograph by Paul Diamond.)

INTRODUCTION

The 2001–2002 basketball season was, arguably, the most exciting in University of Pittsburgh history. It was certainly the most surprising. Picked to finish sixth in the Big East Conference's West Division, head coach Ben Howland's Panthers surprised everyone but themselves in winning a school-record 29 games, including a 13-3 mark in Big East play, good for first place in the West. The Panthers then advanced to the championship game of the Big East Tournament for the second straight year and capped the remarkable run by winning a pair of NCAA Tournament games in front of a home crowd at Pittsburgh's Mellon Arena before falling to Kent State in overtime as part of the Sweet Sixteen. This was the program's first venture that far in the NCAA since 1974.

The honors, deservedly, were many for the Panthers. Howland received numerous national Coach-of-the-Year awards and junior point guard Brandin Knight was named the Big East Conference's Co-Player of the Year.

The timing of Pitt's magnificent season could not have been any better. With the basketball program poised to move into the on-campus, 12,500-seat Petersen Events Center in the fall of 2002, the Panthers captivated basketball fans throughout the region during their final season at the 50-year-old Fitzgerald Field House. Sellout crowds became the norm at Fitzgerald in its farewell run, and ticket sales to future Pitt basketball seasons figured to be brisk because of the momentum and groundswell support generated in 2001–2002.

University of Pittsburgh basketball, however, was not always this successful or popular. Indeed, for many years, neighboring Duquesne University enjoyed a larger following around Pittsburgh, and its teams and players were more widely known than those from Pitt. Colorful ESPN football analyst and one-time Pitt sports information director Beano Cook, who graduated from Pitt and was SID at his alma mater during parts of the 1950s and 1960s, once commented, "The attitude at Pitt used to be that basketball was something between football seasons. If we had a good team, it was by accident."

That may have been so, but a more accurate description of Pitt basketball from earlier years might have been that, thanks to the efforts of many fine players and coaches, Panther teams enjoyed occasional periods of success despite what may have been a less-than-totally-committed attitude on the part of the university's administration toward basketball.

In the old days, from roughly 1930 to 1960, Pitt's basketball rosters were filled with young men from western Pennsylvania and surrounding regions. Members of the football team, looking for a way to stay in shape between the end of football season and spring practice, would often walk on to the basketball roster. Long before weight training and conditioning became sophisticated, off-season pursuits, other varsity sports were prime ways for athletes to stay sharp.

Pitt, with the inherent advantage of being located in a major metropolitan area with a sizable television market, accepted a 1981 invitation to join the prestigious Big East Conference the following season. With the invite came unprecedented revenues and exposure from the conference's outstanding television contracts. Pitt basketball entered the television age, and the university realized it had to put its best foot forward to satisfy not only the ticket-buying public but also the Big East Conference. Coaches' salaries were increased dramatically. Fitzgerald Field House's seating capacity was expanded, and its offices were refurbished. A new generation of Pitt basketball fans was born, many of whom had never seen, or paid much attention to, the pre-Big East varieties.

This book brings to life many of the heralded, and not so heralded, figures who have been a part of Pitt basketball. From Ben Printz, the school's first coach in the inaugural season of 1905–1906, to Ben Howland, from East Liberty's Motor Square Garden to the Petersen Events Center, from Charley Hyatt to Charles Smith, from Doc Carlson to Doctor Roy Chipman, and from Billy Knight to Brandin Knight, Pitt basketball has experienced its share of wonderful highs and heartbreaking lows. From the diametrically opposed personalities of coaches Buzz Ridl and his successor, Tim Grgurich, to the stormy peaks and valleys experienced under Paul Evans, who took the Panthers to more postseason tournaments than any coach in school history, University of Pittsburgh basketball has been a part of the Pittsburgh area's sports scene longer than any other notable team with the exception of the Pittsburgh Pirates and the university's very own football Panthers.

One

EARLY YEARS:
DOC AND HIS BOYS

The Western University of Pennsylvania, as the University of Pittsburgh was then known, fielded its first intercollegiate basketball team in 1905–1906. That team finished the season with a rather modest record of two wins and nine losses. Its coach was Benjamin F. Printz (back row, middle). The team's two victories were against Geneva College and West Virginia University. Included in the first year's results was a 30-4 loss to Penn State University on March 5, 1906. (Photograph courtesy of University of Pittsburgh Archives.)

This photograph from March 2002 shows Motor Square Garden in the East Liberty section of Pittsburgh. Earlier in its life, Motor Square Garden was a prime sporting venue for a number of athletics activities in Pittsburgh, and it was one of the early home facilities for University of Pittsburgh basketball. The facility, which appears much the same today as it did in the early 1900s, later housed an automobile dealership for many years. Today, AAA uses it for an office center, and it also contains a Pennsylvania Photograph Drivers License Center. Pitt played many of its basketball games at Motor Square Garden, which is not to be confused with the now defunct Duquesne Gardens closer to the Pitt campus, before Pitt Stadium was built in 1925. The Panthers also played some of their games at old Trees Gym on campus. (Photograph by Image Point Pittsburgh.)

Legendary Pitt basketball coach Dr. Henry Clifford "Doc" Carlson was a regular at Panther football games at Pitt Stadium. Carlson had been an All-America end for the Panthers of 1917 under the direction of head coach Pop Warner. When Carlson played football for the Panthers, Pitt played its home games at nearby Forbes Field, which had been built for baseball's Pittsburgh Pirates. Carlson was the captain of the 1917 football Panthers. (Photograph courtesy of University of Pittsburgh Archives.)

Willie Arture lettered for three seasons (1929–1931) for some of Doc Carlson's earliest Pitt basketball teams. Arture was one of the Panthers' top players from that era. Pitt's teams won 59 games and lost only 11 during those seasons, including a national championship season (1929–1930) in which they went 23-2. (Photograph by R.P. Hay.)

11

The 1927–1928 Pitt Panthers finished the season 21-0, the only team in school history to finish a season with an undefeated record. The Panthers, coached by Doc Carlson (back row, far left), started the season with a Midwestern road swing, captured victories against Michigan, Chicago, Northwestern, and Ohio University, and finished the year with wins at West Virginia University, Washington & Jefferson University, and Penn State University. According to the *Owl*, Pitt's annual, the 1927–1928 Panthers were "universally recognized as national champions, having hung up the best collegiate record in the country." Pitt's toughest test of the season came at home versus the University of Notre Dame, when All-American Charley Hyatt scored a last-second basket to give the Panthers a 24-22 win. Hyatt was only a sophomore that season.

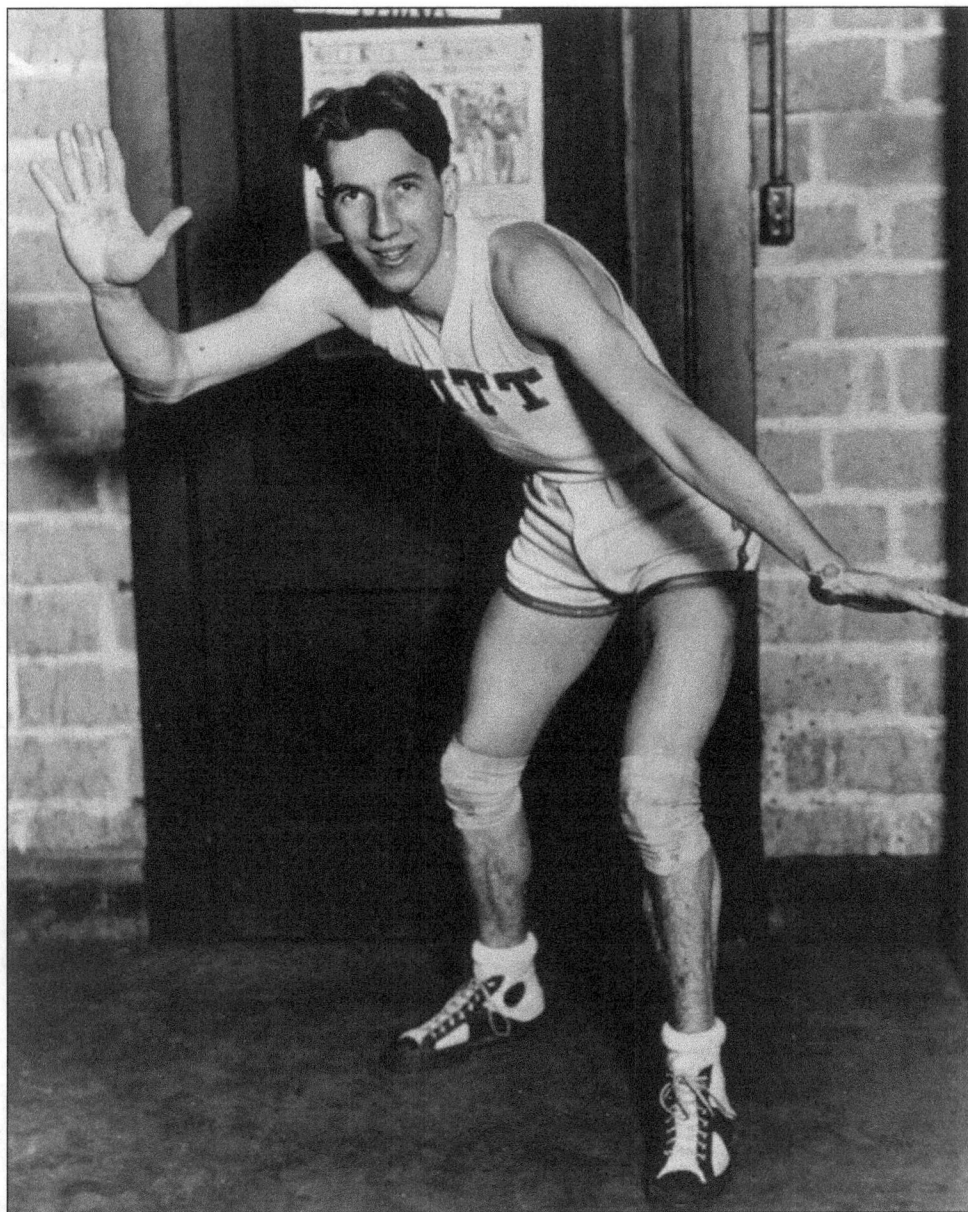

Charley Hyatt was one of Pitt's greatest basketball players of all time and one of its first All-Americans during the highly successful late 1920s. A 6-0 forward from Uniontown, Pennsylvania, Hyatt, nicknamed "Clipper," twice led the nation in scoring during his collegiate career that spanned from 1927 to 1930. He was a consensus first-team All-American in 1929 and 1930. He scored 880 points in his career and led the Panthers to a sparkling 60-7 record over three seasons. Hyatt was named to the Helms Athletic Foundation Hall of Fame and elected to the Naismith Memorial Basketball Hall of Fame in 1959.

A Helms Foundation All-American in 1927–1928, Sykes Reed was a member of Pitt's undefeated national championship team that season. He and fellow All-American Charley Hyatt were two of the Panthers' primary forces during that campaign. Reed was from Braddock, Pennsylvania, the same town that later produced another Pitt basketball All-America great, Billy Knight, in the early 1970s. Reed's backcourt mate on the 1928 team was Stash Wrobleski; Reed and Wrobleski had been high school teammates in Braddock. In later years, Doc Carlson named both Reed and Hyatt to his all-time Pitt Pavilion Team, the name that referred to the Panthers' home basketball facility from 1925 to 1951.

Claire Cribbs, a guard/center from Jeannette, Pennsylvania, was a consensus All-American in 1934 and 1935. He was also named to the Helms Foundation's first-team All-America squad for the same time period. The Panthers were 36-9 during those two seasons. Cribbs later enjoyed a marvelous coaching career in the Pennsylvania and Ohio high school ranks. Upon Cribbs' death in 1985, the Washington Standard-Observer's Don Hall wrote, "Those of us who saw him play will never forget Claire's exceptional ball handling skills, which would have earned him a job with the Harlem Globetrotters if they had wanted to sign a white player."

Pitt All-American Charley Hyatt (center, wearing suit and tie) paid a visit to campus to mingle with a few of the players from Pitt's 1933–1934 squad. This meeting took place in the locker room of the Pitt Pavilion inside Pitt Stadium. From left to right are William Hughes, Claire Cribbs (an All-American that year and also the following season), Hyatt, N.C. Ochsenhirt, and Charles Hughes. This Pitt team finished the season with a record of 18-4, including one 13-game winning streak.

Joe Garcia was a valuable member of Pitt's basketball teams during the mid- to late 1930s. He played center and was a three-time letterman (1936–1938). The Panthers were 41-28 during Garcia's playing career

Frank Carver was a career member of Pitt's athletics department. He graduated from the University of Pittsburgh in 1931 and became the school's athletics publicity director almost immediately. He became athletics director at his alma mater in 1959 and served in that capacity through the 1968–1969 academic calendar year. Carver was responsible for appointing basketball coach Bob Timmons in 1953.

A native Pittsburgher, Don Smith was another one of Doc Carlson's All-America players before World War II. He was a consensus first-team NCAA and Helms Foundation All-America selection for the 1932–1933 season. The Panthers went 17-5 in Smith's final year. Smith later became a practicing dentist in the Pittsburgh area. Claire Cribbs, a teammate of Smith's in the late 1930s, once told Pittsburgh sports author Jim O'Brien, "He [Smith] must have made a pact with the devil. Don Smith never gets old."

The 1940–1941 Pitt basketball team remains the only club in school history to play in what has come to be known as the NCAA Final Four. Pitt defeated North Carolina 26-20 but lost to Wisconsin 36-30 in games played in Madison, Wisconsin. Every member of the team graduated from Pitt, and each man also represented the United States in World War II. "Going to war and fighting, if it came to that, was accepted," said team member Ed Raymond. "It was the right thing to do." From left to right are the following: (front row) Harry Matthews, Sid Silverman, John Swacus, and Bob Artman; (middle row) George Kocheran, Mel Port, Sam Milanovich, Jim Klein, Ed Strall, and Ed Raymond; (back row) head manager Bill Rial, Larry Paffrath, Ed Mastin, Paul Lohmyer, Clair Malarkey, and head coach Doc Carlson.

Bill Cieply played forward and lettered three times for the Panthers during the 1940s. Cieply typified many of the Pitt basketball players who played for Doc Carlson during those days—undersized, but tough and aggressive. One of Carlson's teams was ultimately nicknamed the "Tiny Toughies." (Photograph by Newman-Schmidt Studios.)

A physician by profession, Doc Carlson was a colorful, eccentric, gregarious personality. He was Pitt's basketball coach from 1922 to 1951 and brought some rather unconventional training methods to his trade. Carlson, who was the director of Pitt's Student Health Services, liked to feed ice cream to his players at halftime of games. This mid-1940s photograph shows Carlson doing just that. This picture once appeared in *Look* magazine. "I don't inspire these kids," Carlson was fond of saying. "They inspire me." (Photograph courtesy of University of Pittsburgh Archives.)

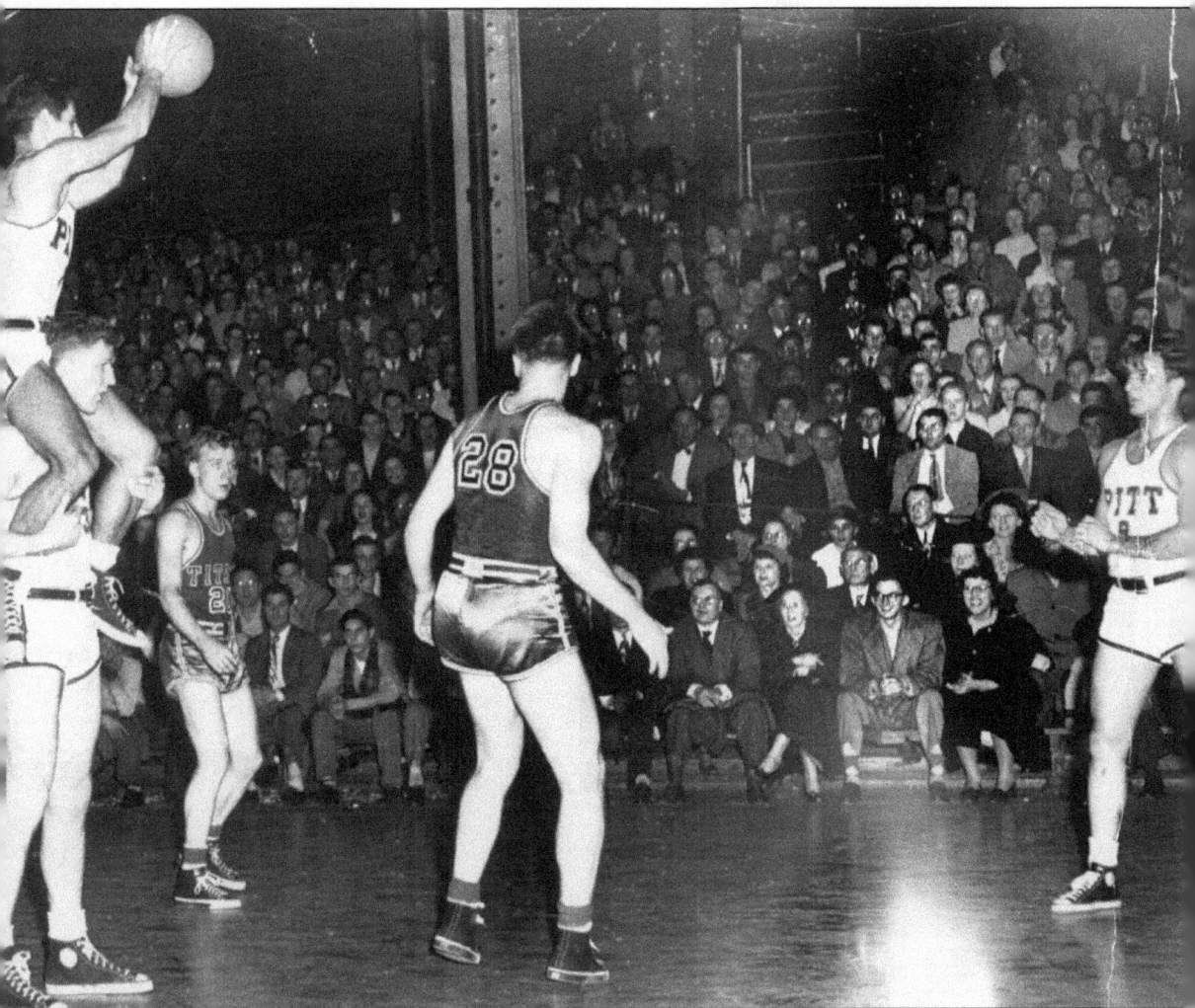

Lou "Bimbo" Cecconi (on shoulders) and Ted Geremsky (hoisting Cecconi) were only following orders relayed to them by Pitt's master showman basketball coach, Doc Carlson, when they pulled this stunt in a game against Westminster College at the Pitt Pavilion in the late 1940s. Explained Cecconi: "We were out in San Francisco and went to the Cow Palace to see the Harlem Globetrotters. They were doing all sorts of things—playing baseball, getting up on each others' shoulders, and throwing the ball around, crazy stuff like that. I remember Carlson telling us at the game, 'We're doing some of those things when we get home.' I thought he was joking." He was not. Carlson had tipped off Westminster's coach prior to the game, so the stunt went off without a hitch or protest.

Oland "DoDo" Canterna was a Pitt basketball letter winner from 1945 to 1949. He was one of more than 100 former Panther basketball players who were in attendance for a series of activities surrounding the final college basketball game played at Fitzgerald Field House on March 2, 2002.

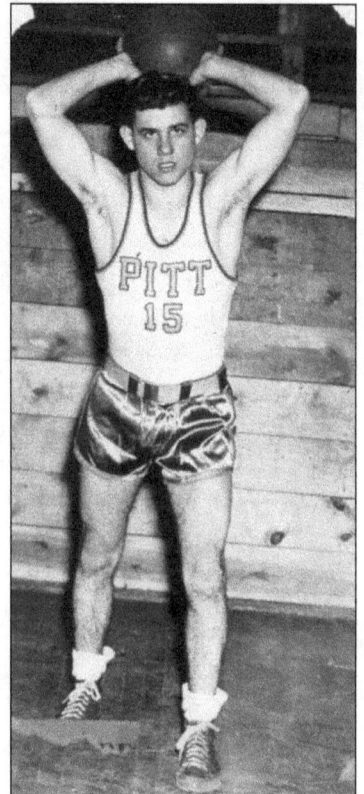

The 1944–1945 Panthers were called the "Phantoms." They finished the season with a record of 8-4, and one of their key players was 5-foot, 8-inch, 155-pound Nate Apple. Apple was from Ford City, Pennsylvania, and had failed to make his high school basketball team. Apple persevered, however, and went on to enjoy a fine college career at Pitt. He later became a dentist. In fact, Apple was a student in Pitt's dental school while playing his final season. He liked to practice dentistry on some of his teammates.

University of Pittsburgh chancellor John Bowman (far right) congratulates coach Doc Carlson (partially hidden) and three of his players following a big win against Ohio State during the 1940s. From left to right are Nate Apple, Sam David, and Bill Cieply. Both Pitt Stadium and Pitt's most familiar campus landmark, the Cathedral of Learning, were built during Bowman's term as chancellor. He is also remembered, though, for his much-publicized difference of philosophy with Pitt's very successful and longtime (1924–1938) football coach Dr. John Bain "Jock" Sutherland. Sutherland resigned as Pitt's coach following the 1938 football season. Bowman remained as chancellor, and Pitt football slumped during the ensuing years.

Sam David was a fine shooting guard who twice led the Panthers in scoring (1946–1947 and 1948–1949). His coach, Doc Carlson, named him to his all-time Pitt Pavilion team at the time of the pavilion's closing after the 1950–1951 season. Sam David went on to become an ordained priest in the Orthodox Church. His son, Joey, lettered for the Panthers from 1983 to 1986. Father and son attended Pitt basketball games at Fitzgerald Field House during the 1970s and early 1980s. (Photograph by Newman-Schmidt Studios.)

Fr. Sam David (far left) is shown with his son, Joey, who is holding his son, Jeremy. Joey's wife, Sandy, and his mother, Janet, complete the family picture. Sam David died in 1999. Joey eventually opened his own physical therapy and sports medicine center in suburban Pittsburgh and became the boys' basketball coach at Mount Lebanon High School. "He [Joey] comes from great stock," Pitt basketball broadcaster Dick Groat once said. "His dad, Sam, was one of my boyhood heroes when I followed the Pitt team when I was growing up."

This was how the Pitt Pavilion appeared in the fall of 1992, more than 40 years after Pitt had played its last basketball game there. Located inside Pitt Stadium, to the left of Gate 1, the pavilion was Pitt's home court from 1925 through the 1950–1951 season. High school basketball tournament games were also played at the Pitt Pavilion during its run. After the pavilion closed for organized basketball, it was used for recreational basketball, among other things. The Pitt band used the pavilion for practices during the 1950s and later utilized the space as a gathering area prior to football games. The Pittsburgh Civic Light Opera used the facility for rehearsals. The Pittsburgh Rens of the old American Basketball League (ABL) used the pavilion as its preseason training camp facility in the early 1960s. The Pitt Pavilion became a memory in 1995, when ground was broken on its site for construction of the new Duratz Center at Pitt Stadium.

Steve Shuber came to the University of Pittsburgh from Butler, Pennsylvania. He was a member of Doc Carlson's Panther teams from 1942 to 1947.

The 1948–1949 Pitt basketball team finished the season with a record of 12-13. In the back row, on the far left wearing a coat and tie, is Doc Carlson. This Panther team had its ups and downs; it had a six-game winning streak early in the season followed by an eight-game losing streak. This photograph was taken in the bleachers at the Pitt Pavilion and includes Lou "Bimbo" Cecconi (front row, far left), DoDo Canterna (next to Cecconi), Mort Lerner (front row, far right), and Ted Geremsky (middle row, fourth from the left).

During a 1949 trip to California, where they played games against the University of California, Stanford University, Loyola Marymount University, and UCLA, members of the Pitt basketball travel party took some time to visit with some Hollywood legends. Jack Benny (front row, wearing a scarf), his wife, Mary Livingston (to Benny's left), and Claudette Colbert (to his right) mingled with the Panthers. At the extreme left is Rochester, Benny's aide-de-camp. To his right are Panther players Bimbo Cecconi and Mort Lerner. Doc Carlson is in the far right of the back row.

Construction continued in the spring and summer of 1951 on the new Memorial Field House on the Pitt campus. The building was the proud project of Pitt's director of athletics at the time, Capt. Tom Hamilton. Its primary objective was to provide an indoor practice facility for the Pitt football team. It was eventually renamed Fitzgerald Field House in honor of Rufus H. Fitzgerald, Pitt's chancellor at the time of the facility's opening.

Ground was broken for the University of Pittsburgh's new Memorial Field House in the winter of 1950–1951. Included in the photograph are Tom Hamilton, director of athletics (far left, holding a shovel), Rufus H. Fitzgerald, university chancellor (middle, with his head down and hands in his pockets), David L. Lawrence (next to Fitzgerald), and an unidentified man digging. At the time this photograph was taken, Lawrence was the mayor of Pittsburgh. One of the most powerful politicians in Pennsylvania history, Lawrence later became governor of the state. A campus building at Pitt now bears his name. Memorial Field House was open for business in the winter of 1951–1952, and the Panthers used it as their home basketball facility for 50 years.

Tom Hamilton was Pitt's director of athletics who presided over what was originally called Memorial Field House. Hamilton had been a star athlete at the U.S. Naval Academy and had served his country, for a time, as commanding officer of the aircraft carrier USS *Enterprise*. Wrote Thomas C. Hansen in the *NCAA News*: "Few men have contributed so widely. Fewer still have earned his awards and accolades, all richly deserved." Hamilton served as Pitt's football coach for the 1951 season and then for part of the 1954 campaign.

Dick Deitrick played for the Panthers from 1952 to 1954, but basketball was not his only sport on campus. He also played football during that era, and one of his teammates and best friends was Pro and College Football Hall of Fame linebacker Joe Schmidt. Deitrick went on to medical school and eventually practiced in the Pittsburgh area. (Photograph by Vinard Studios.)

Doc Carlson celebrates with his players following the Panthers' 74-72 defeat of West Virginia on February 26, 1951, in the final college basketball game played at the Pitt Stadium Pavilion. Pitt won the game on a shot by Scott Phillips in the closing seconds. A dance for Pitt students was staged on the basketball court following the game. Pitt and West Virginia, two old rivals separated by only 70 miles of Interstate 79, have a history of closing out sporting venues with competitions against the other. Pitt upset the Mountaineers 92-87 in the last game played at the old West Virginia University Field House in Morgantown in 1970. On November 10, 1979, the Pitt football team, quarterbacked by freshman Dan Marino, beat West Virginia 24-17 in the last college football game played at old Mountaineer Field. As it turned out, the 2001–2002 Panthers closed down Fitzgerald Field House by defeating West Virginia on March 2, 2002. (Photograph courtesy of University of Pittsburgh Archives.)

The University of Pittsburgh-Duquesne University basketball rivalry has been an on-again, off-again series that has rarely been dull. The two city universities are located only a few miles apart along Pittsburgh's Forbes Avenue. Pitt and Duquesne were bitter rivals in football, basketball, hockey, and even boxing during the 1930s. Unfortunately, some of the pugilistic skills spilled over into the basketball and hockey games, and the universities decided to suspend the basketball series. In fact, Pitt and Duquesne never met on the basketball court during the 1940s. This photograph was taken during a Pitt-Duquesne game played at the Pitt Pavilion in the late 1930s. (Photograph courtesy of University of Pittsburgh Archives.)

Two

THE BOB TIMMONS ERA

Pitt's 1958–1959 basketball team included, from left to right, the following: (front row) assistant coach Lou Iezzi, Bill Mauro, Dick Bickel, Don Hennon, Howard Lockhart, Bill Shay, and manager Harry Peterson; (middle row) Nick Sutyak, Dick Falenski, Darwin Smith, Reid Crookston, Bill Zito, Eliot Maravich, John Mesher, and Lloyd Simpson; (back row) Dave Sawyer, John Fridley, Francis Kondrad, Don Keller, Paul Lazor, Ron Maser, and head coach Bob Timmons.

Bob Timmons succeeded Doc Carlson as the University of Pittsburgh's basketball coach in 1953. He served as the Panthers' head coach through the 1967–1968 season. A Pitt graduate, Timmons did not play basketball in college. He did, however, letter for the football Panthers while playing for Jock Sutherland during the 1930s. He earned two football letters. Timmons had his coaching start as an assistant football coach; he actually coached the basketball team at the same time he was a member of Pitt's football coaching staff. As basketball coach, Timmons led the Panthers to three NCAA Tournament berths (1957, 1958, and 1963) and to a National Invitation Tournament (NIT) appearance in 1964. He resigned following the 1967–1968 season. "Timmons was one of the fine men in the game, and he will be missed," wrote the Owl. "Coaching was getting to be no fun anymore," Timmons remarked. He was replaced by Charles "Buzz" Ridl.

34

Rufus H. Fitzgerald was Pitt's chancellor from 1945 to 1955. Fitzgerald was 54 years old when he took office. He had been provost at Pitt under his predecessor, John Bowman. A graduate of Guilford College in North Carolina, Fitzgerald had once been director of athletics at the University of Tennessee. Fitzgerald presided over one of Pitt's most impressive periods of growth, including a dramatic increase in enrollment during the period after World War II and construction of Pitt's basketball facility, which eventually bore his name.

Pitt's starting lineup from the 1954–1955 season posed for this photograph at Memorial Field House. From left to right are Frank Zimovan, Joe Fenwick, Ed Pavlick, Bob Lazor, and John Riser. Lazor and Riser were both sophomores that season, and each went on to score more than 1,000 points during their careers. This Pitt team finished the season with a record of 10-16. (Photograph courtesy of University of Pittsburgh Archives.)

Fans of western Pennsylvania basketball knew all about Don Hennon when he arrived at Pitt in the late 1950s. He had been a high school star at Wampum High School, where he was coached by his father, L. Butler Hennon. Baseball slugger Dick Allen had also played high school basketball for the elder Hennon at Wampum.

Julius Pegues puts up a shot against Duquesne during the Panthers' 71-49 Steel Bowl loss to Duquesne on December 10, 1955. The game was played at Memorial Field House. Pegues, who came to Pitt from Tulsa, Oklahoma, was the first African-American basketball player to reach 1,000 career points at Pitt. Pegues finished his collegiate career with 1,047 points from 1955–1958. (Photograph courtesy University of Pittsburgh Archives.)

Basketball was not the only event staged at Fitzgerald Field House. An occasional banquet or assembly was held within its walls. Entertainer Bob Hope once made an appearance at the facility and was reported to have said that he had never been in such a big barn. This photograph, taken from the area familiar to Pitt fans as the student seating section, looks across the playing court (covered with a protective surface) in the direction of the reserved seat area. Wrestling matches, volleyball matches, gymnastics competitions, and indoor track meets have also been held at Fitzgerald Field House. The facility also once hosted the NCAA Wrestling Championships. (Photograph by Harry Newman.)

Pitt's Don Hennon puts up a shot against Duquesne's Red Ryan in the Panthers' 71-56 Steel Bowl championship game victory versus the Dukes on December 13, 1958, at the Pitt Field House. The Duquesne player on the far right of the photograph is Ned Twyman, the brother of NBA standout Jack Twyman. Hennon utilized a variety of set shots, jumpers, and running hooks throughout his amazing career with the Panthers.

Bill Mauro played his scholastic basketball at Pittsburgh's North Catholic High School before enrolling at Pitt. He lettered for three seasons (1958–1960), including his sophomore year (1957–1958), when the Panthers lost to Miami University of Ohio in the first round of the NCAA Tournament. A backcourt mate to All-American Don Hennon, Mauro led the Panthers in free throw percentage (87.8) as a senior.

A six-foot, five-inch center from Beaver, Pennsylvania, John Mills led the Panthers in scoring (13.9) as a senior during the 1959–1960 season. He was the first player other than Don Hennon to lead Pitt in that department since Hennon had taken the honor for the three previous seasons. Mills also had the team's best field goal percentage (47.2) during his junior year. (Photograph by John L. Alexandrowicz.)

John Riser was a three-time letterman (1955–1957) for the Panthers and ranks as a member of its basketball 1,000-Point Club. Riser came to Pittsburgh from Washington, Pennsylvania. He scored 1,164 points during his collegiate career and averaged 15.3 points per game as a senior in 1956–1957, when Pitt advanced to the NCAA Tournament.

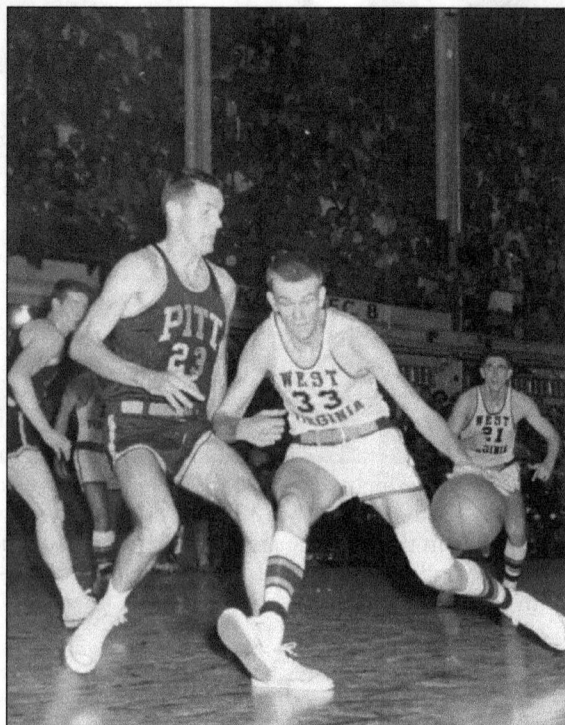

Panther Joe Fenwick has the unenviable challenge of trying to guard West Virginia University's colorful All-American, Hot Rod Hundley, at the January 29, 1955 game in Morgantown. The Mountaineers won 88-74. Pitt has played more basketball games against West Virginia than it has versus any other foe. (Photograph courtesy of West Virginia University Sports Communications Office.)

Dave Sauer (No. 23), Calvin Sheffield (No. 31), and Brian Generalovich (No. 51) all made significant contributions during their careers at the University of Pittsburgh. All three were important contributors to Pitt's 1963 NCAA and 1964 NIT squads. Both Sheffield and Generalovich belong to Pitt's 1,000-Point Club. Sauer went on to become a teacher. Sheffield owned and operated several funeral homes, and Generalovich became a dentist.

A six-foot, three-inch forward from East Meadow, New York, Ben Jinks was a member of Pitt's 1962–1963 NCAA Tournament team. He was also one of the first African-American basketball players at Pitt, following Julius Pegues (1956–1958) and joining teammate Calvin Sheffield (1962–1964). Jinks led the 1960–1961 Panthers in scoring with 13 points per game.

Irwin, Pennsylvania's Chuck Hursh was a three-time letterman (1958–1960) under coach Bob Timmons. A six-foot, four-inch guard, Hursh led the Panthers in rebounding (9.2) as a sophomore and in field goal percentage (49.50) during his junior season. Hursh was a member of Pitt's 1957–1958 NCAA Tournament team.

Guard Dave Roman was a starting guard for the Panthers' NCAA Tournament club of 1962–1963. Roman came to Pittsburgh from Johnstown, Pennsylvania, and led the team in scoring as a junior. In one memorable moment from that season, a basket Roman made was disallowed, for which he is best remembered. In a home game against West Virginia, Roman hit what appeared to be a game-winning shot at the buzzer, but the basket was waved off because another Panther had called timeout. The Panthers lost the game by one point.

A six-foot, six-inch center from Uniontown, Pennsylvania, Paul Krieger was a member of two postseason tournament teams (1963 NCAA and 1964 NIT) during his playing career at the University of Pittsburgh. Krieger, a tough man inside and under the boards, led the Panthers in rebounding during each of those two winning seasons.

43

Brian Generalovich first saw the Pitt campus when his Farrell High School Steelers won WPIAL (Western Pennsylvania Interscholastic Athletic League) and PIAA (Pennsylvania Interscholastic Athletic Association) basketball championships at the Pitt Field House in the late 1950s. He had been a star football and basketball player at Farrell, a sports-crazy town north of Pittsburgh and close to the Ohio border. He had a fine career at Pitt and played one season of football while attending dental school. However, it is basketball for which he is best remembered. "He can't be stopped one-on-one," said West Virginia University coach George King.

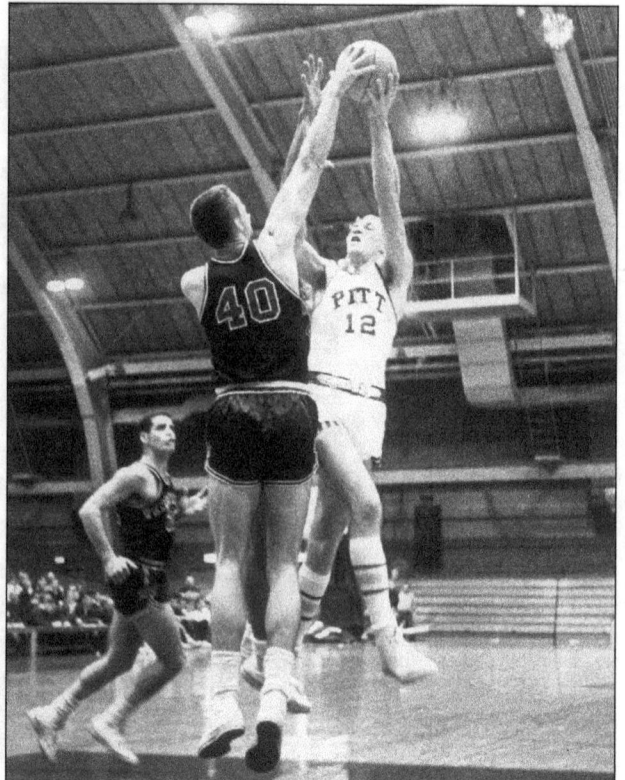

Pitt's Jim LaValley (No. 12) battles for a rebound with the University of Pennsylvania's John Hellings during the Quakers' 75-65 win against the Panthers at the Pitt Field House on December 27, 1965. Observe how the end-zone bleachers are rolled back, not down, a common sight at Panther home games during the mid-1960s. By 2002, Pennsylvania held a 7-5 series edge against Pitt, its intrastate rival from the western part of the state.

Panther All-American Don Hennon battles Westminster College's Chuck Davis for a loose ball in this photograph from a 1960 game at Westminster. The Panthers won this game 75-61. Pitt and Westminster played each other on a regular basis until the early 1970s. Hennon remains one of Pitt's all-time greats. He scored 31 points in his collegiate debut as a sophomore in a road game against North Carolina State University. On December 21, 1957, Hennon scored a school-record 45 points in an 87-84 double-overtime victory against Duke University at the Pitt Field House. He was a two-time All-American and was the first player in Pitt history to have his jersey number retired. During the same time that Hennon was scoring so many points for the Pitt basketball team, Dr. Jonas Salk was busy in research at Pitt, developing the polio vaccine. Beano Cook, Pitt sports information director, wanted to arrange a publicity shot of Salk and Hennon titled "Pitt's Two Greatest Shotmakers," but was unable to pull off the idea. Hennon, coincidentally, became a doctor himself, a surgeon at Pittsburgh's Passavant Hospital. "I wanted to be a doctor," Hennon once remarked. "I didn't know then that I'd be a surgeon. I never worried about not being 6-6." (Photograph courtesy of Office of Public Information, Westminster College.)

This action photograph came from the Pitt-Westminster College game at the Pitt Field House on January 10, 1968. The Panthers lost this game to the Titans, 81-72. Westminster, ironically, was coached by Buzz Ridl, who would become Pitt's new basketball coach after this season. Pitt players are Charley Hunt (No. 42) and Tony DeLisio (No. 32). George Zepernick is the Westminster player handling the ball.

Jerry Causer, a rugged six-foot, five-inch center from Johnstown, Pennsylvania, lettered for the Panthers during Buzz Ridl's first two seasons at the University of Pittsburgh. In 1968–1969, Causer's 42-percent field goal percentage was best on the team. He and Mike Patcher were the Panthers' primary frontcourt forces in those years.

Pitt's Dick Falenski ponders his next move while West Virginia University's All-American Jerry West flies through the air during action from this January 27, 1960 game at the Pitt Field House. The Mountaineers won this game 76-66. The other West Virginia player (No. 25) is Joe Posch. During the 1960s, games against West Virginia generally drew the largest crowds to the Pitt Field House. During the Jerry West era, however, it did not matter where Pitt played West Virginia: WVU was 6-0 against the Panthers during West's career with the Mountaineers. (Photograph courtesy of West Virginia University Sports Communications Office.)

Pitt's Larry Szykowny and Westminster College's John Fontanella scramble for a loose ball during action from Pitt's 70-69 victory against the Titans, coached by Buzz Ridl, on January 12, 1966, at the Pitt Field House. It was one of only five victories that season for the Panthers, who came out on the short end of the score 17 times, including a 26-point loss at Westminster in the next-to-last game of the regular season. As of 2002, Pitt led the all-time series with Westminster 48-33. Note the bleacher seating in the student section. That section of seats used to be suspended from above. An entirely new student section of seating was installed at Fitzgerald Field House in the late 1970s, and an expanded seating capacity took effect in 1981.

Three

BUZZ RIDL AND FRIENDS

Charles "Buzz" Ridl (foreground) succeeded Bob Timmons as Pitt's basketball coach in 1968. He had been a successful coach at Westminster College, where he had also been an outstanding basketball player. He brought a deliberate, disciplined style of basketball to Pittsburgh. One of his assistant coaches with the Panthers was Tim Grgurich (wearing glasses), who had played at Pitt and had been an assistant to Timmons. One of Ridl's early recruits to Pitt was center Jim Bolla (to Grgurich's right). Grgurich later replaced Ridl at Pitt. Bolla eventually became head women's basketball coach at the University of Nevada Las Vegas.

A 1974 *Sports Illustrated* article referred to him as a "grandfather figure." At age 52, Buzz Ridl guided the Pitt basketball team to an incredible 25-4 record in 1973–1974. "Buzz personifies stability and hard work," said his wife, Betty Ridl, who kept charts of all the games her husband coached. "He is sensible and he doesn't get carried away with all the unrealistic stuff." Ridl, who coached the Panthers for seven seasons (1968–1975), retired from basketball coaching in 1975 and ultimately returned to his alma mater, Westminster College, as an administrator. He died in 1995.

Mike Riggle was a consistent, valuable frontcourt player for the Panthers. He was recruited to Pittsburgh by Bob Timmons and finished his collegiate career under Buzz Ridl. Riggle earned three letters (1969–1971) for the Panthers. He and Charley Hunt were the main forwards for Ridl's earliest Panther squads of the late 1960s.

Kent Scott was one of Buzz Ridl's first Pitt recruits. He came to Pittsburgh by way of Raytown, Missouri. The sharpshooting Scott had a fine career with the Panthers. A three-year starter, he led the team in scoring in both his sophomore and junior seasons. He finished his career with 1,143 points. Blessed with tremendous shooting range and accuracy, one can only wonder how many points Scott would have scored had the three-point basket been in effect during his playing days. He also finished his career with an impressive shooting percentage of 49.9.

Not until the 1969–1970 season were all University of Pittsburgh basketball games, both home and away, broadcast by a commercial radio station in Pittsburgh. Eight years later, the same broadcast team was still behind the microphones. Dean Billick (open collar) was Pitt's sports information director at the time and doubled as color analyst on radio. Bill Hillgrove (peering upward) was, and still is, play-by-play man. This 1978 photograph also shows, to Hillgrove's right, Carlton Neverson, a transfer player who sat out that season. (Photograph by Rich Wilson.)

Mike Paul was another western Pennsylvania schoolboy basketball player who matriculated at the University of Pittsburgh. Paul, however, was not originally a scholarship player. He had a nice career at Baldwin High School and decided to walk on at Pitt when a friend of freshman coach Tim Grgurich encouraged Paul to give it a shot. He did, and Paul became a three-year starter and letterman. He played both shooting guard and small forward.

Pitt fielded either a freshman or junior varsity team for much of the 1960s and part of the 1970s. The team normally played its games as preliminaries to the varsity contests. In this 1971 photograph, Panthers Buzzy Harrison (No. 52) and Chris Jones (No. 12) try to negate the 7-4 frame of North Carolina State University's Tom Burleson in a game played at Fitzgerald Field House. As a senior in 1973–1974, Burleson was the Wolfpack's starting center when North Carolina State defeated Pitt in the NCAA Tournament. (Photograph by Robert Donaldson.)

52

Pitt and West Virginia are old, familiar rivals who have a history of closing out athletics facilities in games pitting the two. This is a wide-angle view of the old West Virginia Field House on the night of March 3, 1970. Pitt upset the Mountaineers 92-87 in the final college basketball game played in the Mountaineers' 42-year-old facility. Said Pitt coach Buzz Ridl the day before the game: "This is the last game in their old gym and ghosts of Jerry West, Mark Workman, and other great stars will be around to haunt us." But it was the Panthers who did the haunting in the final analysis. Pitt appeared spooked in the first half, trailing West Virginia by as many as 19 points, but sophomore guard Kent Scott sparked an amazing second-half turnaround, scoring 23 of his game-high 32 points after intermission to spark Pitt's thrilling comeback victory. Pitt All-American Charley Hyatt, who played in the old West Virginia Field House when it opened in 1928, was in attendance 42 years later to receive a plaque during a special halftime ceremony. (Photograph courtesy of West Virginia University Sports Communications Office.)

Sophomore Ed "Buzzy" Harrison played only one season (1970–1971) of varsity basketball at Pitt, but he was a valuable performer coming off the bench. His biggest game that season was on the night of December 29, 1970, when the Panthers upset the Duquesne Dukes 70-58 in the first round of the Steel Bowl at the Civic Arena in Pittsburgh. Harrison scored a game-high 25 points, including 11 of 12 free throws, to go along with 8 rebounds. The victory also snapped Duquesne's 20-game winning streak at the Civic Arena. The Duquesne player in the photograph is Mike Barr.

College students have always been known for silly pranks, but Pitt undergraduates started a unique tradition at basketball games in the late 1960s: tossing fish onto the court to protest a perceived bad call by the officials. In this photograph from the January 14, 1970 Pitt-West Virginia University basketball game, longtime Pitt athletics groundskeeper and resident funnyman Leo "Horse" Czarnecki displays a fish someone threw onto the court during the Panthers' 67-66 loss to the Mountaineers. "They used to throw eels," said Czarnecki. "But they were a lot messier to try to clean up." (Copyright Ross Catanza/Pittsburgh Post-Gazette, 2002 All rights reserved. Reprinted with permission.)

54

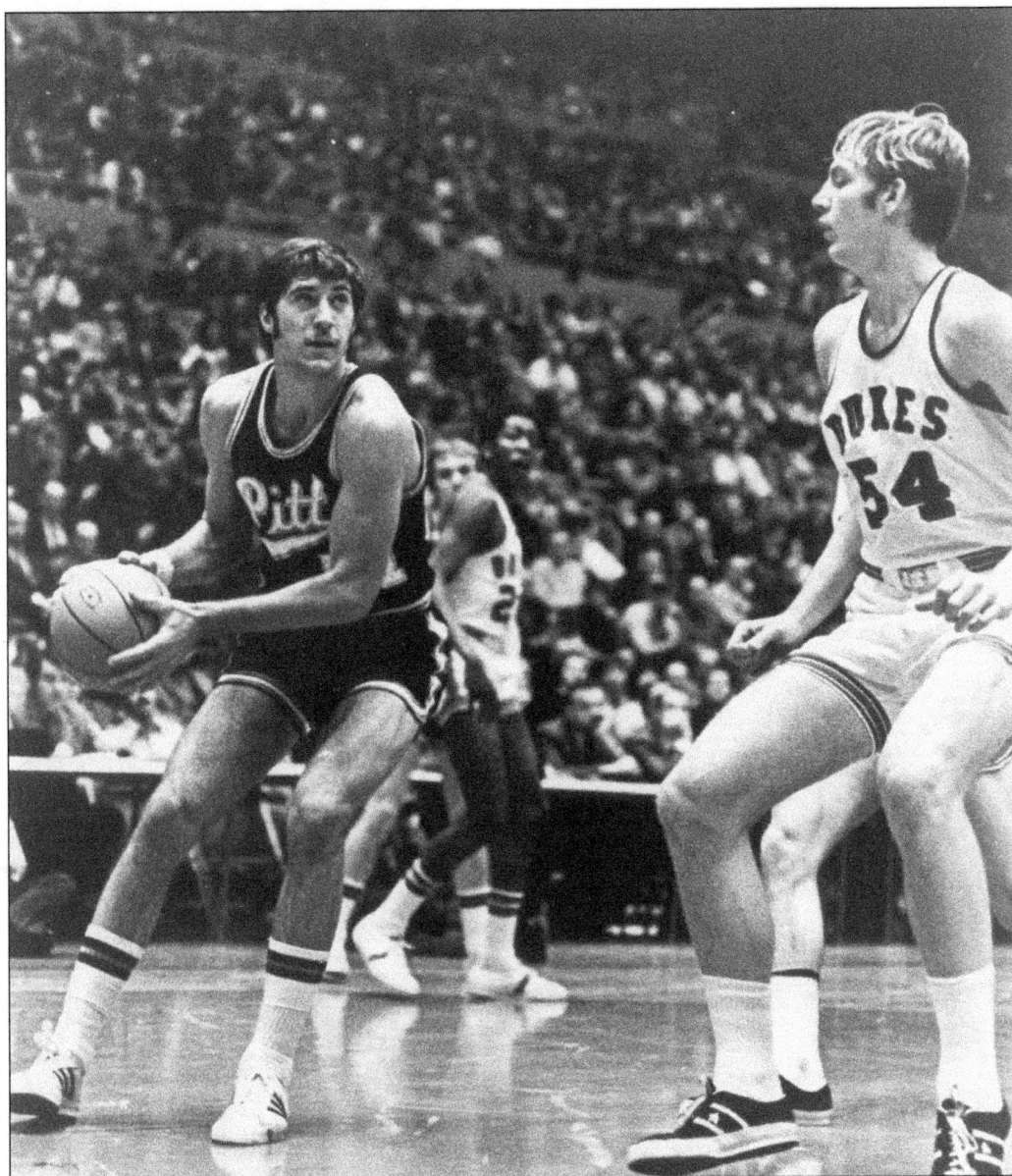

Pitt's Paul O'Gorek prepares to make his move against Duquesne's Garry Nelson (No. 54) in the 1970 Pitt-Duquesne University Steel Bowl game at the Civic Arena. The Panthers upset the favored Dukes 70-58, setting up a meeting with undefeated and top-ranked UCLA the next night in the finals. Nelson's twin brother, Barry Nelson, also played for the Dukes, in an era when many of the Pitt-Duquesne combatants were Pittsburgh-area products. The loss was especially bitter for the Dukes to swallow. Their program enjoyed much greater support, fan interest, and media coverage than did Pitt's during the late 1960s. This was Pitt coach Buzz Ridl's third season with the Panthers, and he understood the significance of the victory. "This was my biggest win at Pitt," Ridl offered. "Our defense was something tonight." Pitt limited Duquesne to 35 percent shooting from the floor. The Duquesne player in the background is Jarrett Durham, who later became the head coach at Robert Morris College. After the loss to Pitt, the Dukes went on to win 15 consecutive games.

Legendary UCLA coach John Wooden made his only collegiate coaching appearance in Pittsburgh in 1970, when he brought his national champion Bruins to town for the Steel Bowl. UCLA defeated William & Mary in the opening round, setting up a game against the Panthers for the tournament championship. UCLA won this game on December 30, 1970, before a Civic Arena crowd of 13,535, at the time the largest crowd ever to watch a college basketball game at the nine-year-old arena. In this photograph, Pitt's Billy Downes drives for a layup. Bill Sulkowski (No. 54) waits for a possible rebound. This UCLA team featured Sidney Wicks, Curtis Rowe, Henry Bibby, and Steve Patterson. Rowe and Wicks each scored 26 points in the Bruins' 77-64 win.

Pitt's Mike Paul (right) and UCLA's Steve Patterson appear to be squaring off during the finals of the 1970 Steel Bowl at the Civic Arena. The Bruins were 13-point victors against the upstart Panthers, and UCLA went on to win another national championship that season. Pitt finished the 1970–1971 campaign with a record of 14-10. For basketball trivia buffs, Patterson was UCLA's starting center after Lew Alcindor (Kareem Abdul-Jabbar) and before Bill Walton.

Kent Scott makes a pass to Paul O'Gorek (No. 50) in this early-1970s game against an unidentified opponent at Fitzgerald Field House. Scott and O'Gorek were among coach Buzz Ridl's first recruits to Pittsburgh. Edwards, a Pittsburgher who had been a fine football and basketball player at Fifth Avenue High School, later served as an assistant coach at Pitt under Tim Grgurich. Edwards also served as an assistant to Grgurich at the University of Nevada Las Vegas in 1994–1995 and replaced Grgurich, finishing out that season as the Rebels' interim coach, when illness forced Grgurich to give up his coaching duties that year.

The man seated at the press table to the left of visiting player No. 13 was longtime Fitzgerald Field House public address announcer Harold Neff, whose familiar voice was heard at Pitt football games at Pitt Stadium throughout the 1960s and much of the 1970s. Neff also performed PA duties for WPIAL high school basketball playoff games.

At 6 feet, 10 inches tall, Lucius Keese, a junior college transfer from Largo, Florida, was at the time of his enrollment the tallest basketball player in Pitt history. He did not play much during his years at Pitt (1973–1975), but the good-natured Keese was a fan favorite at Fitzgerald. Keese had a standing reach of nine feet and wore size 17 tennis shoes. A subsequent generation of Pitt students came to know Keese from his work as a security guard at the Original Hot Dog Shop in Oakland, a popular campus hangout.

The University of North Carolina's Bobby Jones (No. 34) and Pitt's Carl Morris (No. 22) battle for the ball in this photograph from the Panthers' 1971–1972 home opener played on December 4, 1971, at Fitzgerald Field House. Other Tar Heel players in the picture are Ambridge, Pennsylvania's Dennis Wuycik (No. 44), and Bob McAdoo (No. 35). Two other North Carolina starters that night, Steve Previs from Bethel Park and George Karl of Penn Hills, were from the Pittsburgh area. This was Dean Smith's only coaching appearance at Fitzgerald Field House. The Tar Heels won 90-75, spoiling Billy Knight's Fitzgerald debut for Pitt.

One of the greatest teams in school history, the 1973–1974 Panthers registered a record of 25-4, including a school-record 22-game winning streak. The Panthers lost their opening game of the season at West Virginia University before taking their next 22 straight. The streak was snapped in a 66-64 last-second loss at Penn State, followed by a loss at South Carolina. Pitt ended the regular season with a win against West Virginia at Fitzgerald Field House and then beat Saint Joseph's (Philadelphia) and Furman in the NCAA Tournament before bowing to North Carolina State University. From left to right are the following: (front row) Mike Jones, Bob Shrewsbury, Ken Wagoner, Kirk Bruce, Sam Fleming, Tom Richards, Frank Boyd, Scott Nedrow, Lew Kelly, and trainer Bob Mangine; (back row) assistant coach Fran Webster, head coach Buzz Ridl, Lew Hill, Wayne Talbot, Greg McBride, Jim Bolla, John Endsley, Scott Stephens, Mark Disco, Willie Kelly, Keith Starr, Billy Knight, manager Lefty Booth, and assistant coach Tim Grgurich.

One of Pitt basketball's all-time greats, Billy Knight eventually had his jersey number retired during a special ceremony at Fitzgerald Field House on February 20, 1989. Knight came to Pitt following an illustrious scholastic career at Braddock High School, starting a trend under Buzz Ridl, and continuing under Tim Grgurich, of attracting many of the top Pittsburgh-area high school talents to Pitt. "There are a lot of nice people in the world," said his coach, Buzz Ridl, "But none any finer than Billy Knight." Knight led the Panthers in both scoring and rebounding in all three seasons (1972–1974) he played for the Panthers. He went on to enjoy an 11-year professional basketball career and later served as general manager of the NBA's Memphis Grizzlies.

Mickey Martin was Billy Knight's running mate at forward for three seasons, including the memorable 25-4 campaign of 1973–1974. Martin graduated from Baldwin High School in suburban Pittsburgh, where one of his classmates and basketball teammates was future Pitt football player and NFL head coach Dave Wannstedt. Martin was the Panthers' second-leading scorer and rebounder in 1973–1974. This photograph shows Martin in action against Davidson at Fitzgerald Field House on January 10, 1973. The Panthers lost 76-73. (Photograph by Michael Chikiris.)

Junior college transfer Lew Hill looks to dish off the ball against Penn State during the Panthers' 83-61 victory against the Nittany Lions on January 27, 1974, at Fitzgerald Field House. This was Pitt's 15th straight win; it would reach 22 that season. Hill played two seasons (1973–1975) for the Panthers, usually in reserve roles. Pitt made postseason tournament appearances in each of those seasons. Hill had come to Pitt following two seasons at Ferrum Junior College in Virginia.

This photograph was from the March 16, 1974 NCAA East Region final game between Pitt and North Carolina State University. The Elite Eight game was played at Reynolds Coliseum in Raleigh, North Carolina, the Wolfpack's home court. In what turned out to be his final game as a Panther, Billy Knight grabs a rebound in the team's 100-72 loss. A victory in this game would have put the Panthers in the Final Four, opposite UCLA. Instead, North Carolina State went on to defeat the Bruins in a memorable semifinal game before beating Marquette to capture the 1974 national championship. (Photograph courtesy of University of Pittsburgh Archives.)

Billy Knight, left, watches as his younger brother, Terry Knight, spins a basketball inside Fitzgerald Field House in the mid-1970s. When Billy left Pitt after the 1973–1974 season, Terry stepped in from 1974 to 1979. "I want to make it like he [Billy] did," Terry once said. A two-year starter at small forward, Terry helped lead the Panthers to 34 wins during those two seasons. Billy and Terry were two of eleven children in the Knight family.

Tom Richards once scored 63 points in a game for Moon Township High School. He brought his game to Pittsburgh in 1972 and was a four-year letterman and three-year starter at point guard. He led the 1973–1974 NCAA team in assists and teamed with Kirk Bruce to give the Panthers a pair of dead-eye shooting guards. "We had a good team, led by Billy Knight and Mickey Martin," Richards once said. "We felt unbeatable when we were at the [Fitzgerald] Field House." Indeed, the Panthers stretched their home winning streak to 27 games in 1975, when Richards canned a 40-foot heave at the buzzer to beat Ohio University. Later a successful business executive, Richards retired from his position as president of Ameritech at the age of 45.

The 1973–1974 season was a magical one for the University of Pittsburgh and the city of Pittsburgh. The 25-4 basketball season capped an unbelievable year for Panther athletics; the football team, led by first-year coach Johnny Majors, posted Pitt's first winning season in 10 years. The most distinctive aspect of the basketball team that season was the fact that so many of the key players, including all five starters, were from the Pittsburgh area. *Sports Illustrated* ran a feature about the Panthers in one of its 1974 issues, along with the accompanying photograph. Six members of the team assembled at an observation point atop the Mount Washington section of Pittsburgh, with Three Rivers Stadium in the background, for this unique photograph opportunity. From left to right are the following: (front row) Pittsburghers Mickey Martin (Baldwin) and Billy Knight (Braddock); (back row) Tom Richards (Moon Township), Keith Starr (Sewickley), Jim Bolla (Crafton), and Kirk Bruce (Pittsburgh South Hills).

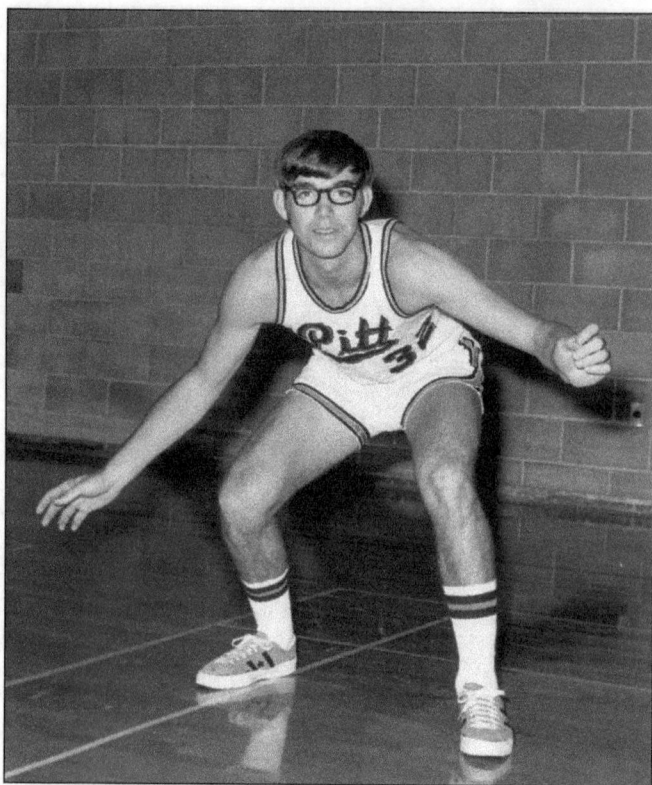

Kenny Wagoner was a fine defensive player and an underrated shooter who was one of the first players off the bench throughout the 1973–1974 basketball season. Wagoner, who came to Pitt from Beaver Falls, Pennsylvania (also the hometown of Joe Namath), eventually became a minister. He was a three-time letterman for the Panthers.

Paul Auslander, known to hordes of Pittsburgh sports fans as "Tiger" Paul, was a Pittsburgher who graduated from Peabody High School. Auslander excited Pitt fans by leading the student section in cheering. He would wear elaborate costumes—pajamas, a tuxedo, or a Santa Claus outfit, for instance—and was a familiar sight on Pittsburgh streets for much of the 1970s and early 1980s. Atlanta Braves owner Ted Turner, after seeing Tiger's act, invited Auslander to Atlanta for a two-week, all-expenses-paid working vacation to lead Braves fans in cheering from atop the dugout at Fulton County Stadium. Auslander died in Nevada in 1993. (Photograph courtesy of University of Pittsburgh Archives.)

University of Pittsburgh basketball player Ralph McClelland (right) grew up on Pittsburgh's North Side and for two years attended Community College of Allegheny County (CCAC), where he played for former Pitt basketball guard Bill Shay. McClelland enrolled at Pitt in 1974. He visited a familiar North Side landmark, Three Rivers Stadium, for this 1975 photograph with another Pittsburgh sports icon, legendary Pittsburgh Pirates broadcaster Bob Prince. Prince broadcast Pirates games from 1948 to 1975. Prince died in 1985. Three Rivers Stadium was imploded in 2001. A parking lot, convenient to both PNC Park (Pittsburgh Pirates) and Heinz Field (Pittsburgh Steelers and Pitt Panthers), now takes up the space Three Rivers Stadium occupied from 1970 to 2001.

Pitt's Melvin Bennett (No. 34) battles West Virginia University's Warren Baker in an ECAC Southern Division game at Fitzgerald Field House on February 12, 1975. The Panthers won 83-77, gaining a measure of revenge for a loss to West Virginia earlier in the season in Morgantown. Pitt's Keith Starr (No. 30) and West Virginia's Jerome Anderson (No. 24) observe from a safe distance. Pitt's home games with West Virginia and Duquesne were generally the top draws during this time period.

Before the Eastern Eight Conference was formed in 1976, the Pitt basketball program played most of its seasons as an independent. The Panthers did, however, play in a conference of sorts in 1974–1975, when they were part of the ECAC's Southern Division. As such, they journeyed to Morgantown, West Virginia, on March 7, 1975, as the top seed. Their opponent was fourth-seeded West Virginia University, host of the tournament. The Panthers lost a bitter 75-73 decision to the Mountaineers and had their hopes of returning to the NCAA Tournament thwarted. Pitt players in this photograph are Melvin Bennett (far left), Jim Bolla (guarding West Virginia's Eartha Faust), and Keith Starr (No. 30). Bennett, a true freshman, had 22 points and 21 rebounds in this game. (Photograph courtesy of West Virginia University Sports Communications Office.)

Pitt's Larry Harris and Kirk Bruce (40) try to decide which player should score the basket during the Panthers' relatively easy 89-64 victory against George Washington University in the consolation game of the 1975 ECAC Southern Division Tournament at the WVU Coliseum in Morgantown, West Virginia. The Panthers had lost to West Virginia the night before, while Georgetown defeated George Washington, setting up this consolation meeting. Pitt's reward for this victory was an invitation to the National Invitation Tournament (NIT), in those days played exclusively at New York City's Madison Square Garden. Pitt defeated Southern Illinois in the opening round, but lost a second-round game against Providence College, coached by Dave Gavitt. Gavitt later became the first commissioner of the Big East Conference. The loss to Providence was the final game in the seven-year coaching tenure of Buzz Ridl, who announced his retirement from coaching in April 1975.

Starting in the mid-1960s, the Civic Arena in Pittsburgh hosted what Pittsburgh basketball fans simply referred to as the "Roundball." The Dapper Dan Roundball Classic was an annual event held in late March or early April and drew tremendous crowds to the arena. The most popular format for the game matched a pair of high school all-star teams from western Pennsylvania in the first game, followed by the main event, the Pennsylvania All-Stars versus the U.S. All-Stars. These members of the 1973–1974 University of Pittsburgh basketball team—all from the Pittsburgh area—were alumni of the Roundball Classic. From left to right are Greg McBride (Pittsburgh), Billy Knight (Braddock), Jim Bolla (Crafton), Keith Starr (Sewickley), Sam Fleming (Pittsburgh), Kirk Bruce (Pittsburgh), Scott Nedrow (Monongahela), Frank Boyd (Pittsburgh), and Tom Richards (Murrysville).

Melvin Bennett's college basketball career with the Panthers ended far too soon for Pitt fans. A powerful six-foot, seven-inch center who had starred at Pittsburgh's Peabody High School, Bennett arrived at Pitt for the 1974–1975 season and become a starter almost immediately. He averaged 10 points and 8 rebounds per game that year, including several outstanding games. Bennett also established a Pitt single-season record by blocking 70 shots. Bennett opted to turn professional after his first season; he was the first-round draft choice of the American Basketball Association's (ABA) Virginia Squires.

Students from Pittsburgh's Schenley High School have never had far to go if they decide to attend the University of Pittsburgh. The background image of Pitt's Cathedral of Learning shows the proximity of the two Oakland landmark institutions. Pitt attracted three basketball players—Wayne Williams, Kelvin Smith and Nathan "Sonny" Lewis—during the mid-1970s. (Photograph by Image Point Pittsburgh.)

Fran Webster, a Slippery Rock University graduate, served as an assistant coach to Buzz Ridl at Westminster College during much of the 1960s. He joined Ridl at Pitt in 1969 and remained with the Panthers as an aide to Ridl's successor, Tim Grgurich. Webster's Pittsburgh tenure ran from 1969 to 1980. His coaching legacy is the "amoeba defense," an ever-changing combination man-to-man and zone defense. For some games at Fitzgerald Field House, Webster positioned himself in the upper balcony and communicated via headphones with the coaches on the bench.

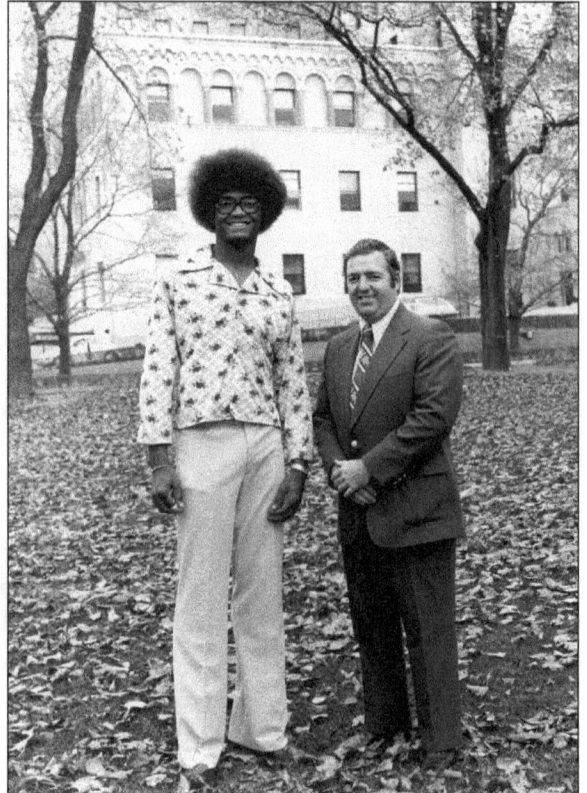

Former University of Pittsburgh All-America basketball player Dr. Don Hennon (right) welcomes freshman center Melvin Bennett to Pitt in the fall of 1974. This photograph was taken on the lawn of Pitt's Cathedral of Learning. The Panthers were 18-11 during Bennett's only season. Pitt basketball media guides in those years often showed a current player with a former Panther in some familiar Pittsburgh setting.

Pittsburgh born, bred, and educated, Tim Grgurich was a part of Pitt basketball from his first day as a college freshman in 1960 until the day he resigned as head coach in 1980. He earned two degrees from Pitt and was a member of two tournament teams as a playmaking guard in the early 1960s. He worked as an assistant coach to both Bob Timmons and Buzz Ridl and was named Pitt's head coach in 1975 at age 33. Fiercely devoted to his players, Grgurich was Ridl's chief recruiter and had begun an impressive record of keeping some of the top high school players in the region in Pittsburgh. A tough disciplinarian, Grgurich demonstrated how far he would go to make his point during his first season as head coach. He suspended several players from Pitt's December 30, 1975 game at Cleveland State because they had accepted free beer samples during a trip to a brewery in Florida earlier in the season. Foul trouble came, and the Panthers were forced to play the final minutes of the Cleveland State game with only four players on the court. Pitt lost 60-56. Grgurich pushed and sometimes scrapped with the administration at Pitt, looking to make improvements in the basketball program. He announced his resignation one day after a two-point loss to Duquesne in the National Invitation Tournament (NIT). His last three Pitt teams—all winners—were a combined 51-34. His overall record was 69-70. "There was nobody, absolutely nobody, who loved Pitt basketball more or who worked harder to make it better than Tim Grgurich," wrote Pittsburgh Post-Gazette sportswriter Bob Smizik, who was an undergraduate student at Pitt along with Grgurich. Grgurich later served for a brief time as the head coach at the University of Nevada Las Vegas, following a long stint as an assistant to Jerry Tarkanian at that university.

Fitzgerald Field House had a new and improved locker room for the men's basketball team in 1973. The room, built in the downstairs portion of the building, was financed by the Pitt Golden Panther Rebounders, an offshoot booster club designed solely for the support of the basketball program. The group held car raffles, sponsored trips to road games, and organized other activities for Pitt alumni, fans, and basketball devotees.

Pitt's Sam Clancy (clutching the basketball) is tied up by Duquesne University's Jesse Hubbard during action from Pitt's 72-65 win against the Dukes at Fitzgerald Field House on February 22, 1978. Clancy, a freshman that year, scored 20 points and grabbed 20 rebounds to help the Panthers avenge an earlier 22-point loss to their city rival. (Photograph by Rich Wilson.)

One of the most popular and productive basketball players in Pitt history, Sam Clancy was a rugged 6-foot, 6-inch, 245-pound forward/center who grew up not too far from the Pitt campus. He was a football and basketball star at Fifth Avenue High School in Pittsburgh. As a high school junior, Clancy led his team to an undefeated season and the Pennsylvania Interscholastic Athletic Association (PIAA) state championship. That season (1975–1976) was the last year for Fifth Avenue High School; it became part of a new high school, Brashear, in 1976. At Pitt, Clancy played on four winning teams and made it to two postseason tournaments. He accumulated more rebounds (1,342) than any player in college basketball during the same four-year period. He is the only player in school history to reach 1,000 career rebounds. He also is a member of Pitt's 1,000-Point Club. "He's Superman in basketball shorts," is how then University of Cincinnati coach Gale Catlett described Clancy following a 24-point, 12-rebound performance as a freshman. Clancy went out for spring football at Pitt in 1980 but gave it up to concentrate on basketball. He never played in the NBA but did enjoy an 11-year career in professional football. He ultimately became the defensive line coach for the National Football League's (NFL) New Orleans Saints. His son, Sam Clancy Jr., had an excellent basketball career at the University of Southern California.

Terry Knight, the younger brother of Pitt All-American Billy Knight, goes up for a shot in this Eastern Eight basketball game against the University of Massachusetts. This game was played early in the 1978–1979 season, Knight's senior year. He teamed with Sam Clancy and Sammie Ellis to give Pitt a relatively short, but very quick and aggressive front line. For much of this season, the Panthers were the leading rebounding team in the nation. Ellis, at six feet, seven inches, was the tallest starter. (Photograph by Rich Wilson.)

Most Pitt fans remember East Point, Georgia's Robert Haygood as one of the quarterbacks during the Panthers' 1976 national championship football season. The Pitt football teams were 8-2 in the games Haygood started, but his gridiron career ended abruptly on September 18, 1976, when he suffered a severe knee injury in a win at Georgia Tech. Haygood did take advantage of the "red shirt" year and came back the following season (1977–1978) as a backup point guard for the basketball team. He played basketball throughout his Pitt career.

74

Larry Harris, one of the most prolific scorers in Pitt basketball history, drives for a layup in a game against Southern Illinois University in the first round of the 1976 Golden Triangle Classic at the Civic Arena. The in-season tournament—known formerly as the Steel Bowl—began in 1951 when the new Pitt Field House opened. The 1976–1977 season was a bitter one for the Panthers and their fans. The team lost a school-record 21 games against only 6 victories. Much was made of the Panthers' incoming freshman class that season, a group that included power forward Michael Rice (adjacent to Harris's right leg) and guard Sonny Lewis (No. 53). Wayne Williams (No. 43) is the other Panther in the picture. Both Lewis and Williams were graduates of Pittsburgh's Schenley High School. The highlight of the 1976–1977 season was a stunning 65-64 upset victory against the nationally ranked Cincinnati Bearcats. Pitt won the game, played at Fitzgerald Field House, when Harris hit a corner jump shot as time expired. The 1976–1977 Panthers also beat Duquesne University 64-56 in Norm Nixon's last home game at the Civic Arena. The Dukes won the Eastern Eight Tournament title six nights after losing to Pitt.

Willie Kelly (right) and George Medich get together for a chat on Pitt's campus in 1975. Kelly came to Pittsburgh on an academic scholarship from Philadelphia's Overbrook High School. He was a key reserve forward on Pitt's great 1973–1974 team and was a part-time starter the next two seasons. Medich, who played football and baseball at Pitt, graduated from Pitt's School of Medicine. He pitched for several teams in the major leagues, including one season (1976) with the Pittsburgh Pirates. George "Doc" Medich still makes his home and works in western Pennsylvania.

A versatile swingman with great quickness and long arms, New York City's Carlton Neverson (No. 24) scored 1,057 points in his career (1978–1981) with the Panthers. As a junior in 1980, he led Pitt in steals, free throw percentage, and field goal percentage. In this photograph, Neverson battles for a loose ball in a victory against St. Bonaventure University.

Nathan "Sonny" Lewis was a schoolyard star in Pittsburgh and well known to area basketball fans during his career at Schenley High School. He arrived at Pitt in 1976 amidst rave billings from fans, coaches, and the media. However, things did not work out for Lewis at Pitt. A phenomenal leaper who thrilled Panther fans with his acrobatic moves to the hoop and stylish slam dunks, the six-foot, one-inch Lewis eventually landed in coach Tim Grgurich's doghouse because of philosophical differences. "Grgurich thought he understood Sonny Lewis," wrote Pittsburgh sportswriter Bob Smizik. "Sonny Lewis thought Tim Grgurich was the man to coach him. Both were wrong. Lewis finished a fine career at Point Park. Tim Grgurich became a different coach." Lewis left Pitt midway through his sophomore season (1977–1978) and transferred to Point Park College in downtown Pittsburgh. He died of a drug overdose not long after his college career ended.

Dave Olinger applies the pressure to a Massachusetts Minuteman in the Panthers' 70-54 win over the University of Massachusetts at Fitzgerald Field House on December 2, 1978. Coming to Olinger's assistance are Sammie Ellis (No. 52) and Carlton Neverson (No. 24). Three weeks later, Pitt beat Massachusetts again 87-68 at the Gator Bowl Tournament in Jacksonville, Florida. The Panthers finished 18-11 that season.

Pitt's Wayne Williams, an excellent defensive player, hounds Duquesne University's excellent point guard, Baron "B.B." Flenory, in the February 22, 1978 Eastern Eight game at Fitzgerald Field House. The Panthers won 72-65, giving them an even series split with the Dukes that season. It was also Senior Night at Pitt.

Sammie Ellis was a scoring forward who had transferred to Pittsburgh from Middle Georgia Junior College in 1978. He looked and was built a lot like NBA star George Gervin. Fortunately, he even played a little bit like Gervin. Ellis had an excellent career at Pitt, spanning two seasons (1978–1980). He was the team's leading scorer in those seasons with 17 points per game. He also was named the Most Valuable Player at that year's Connecticut Mutual Classic, which the Panthers won by defeating the University of Connecticut in the championship game. In this photograph, Ellis goes up for a shot during Pitt's 77-64 win against Villanova University in the semifinals of the Eastern Eight Tournament on March 1, 1979, at the Civic Arena in Pittsburgh. The Panthers lost the title game to Rutgers before a sellout crowd two nights later. Pitt and Villanova met in the semifinals of the Eastern Eight Tournament for three straight years (1978, 1979, and 1980). The Wildcats won the first and third meetings. The annual Eastern Eight event was a smashing success in Pittsburgh. It was held at the Civic Arena for five straight years, 1978–1982, and drew excellent crowds. When Pitt left the Eastern Eight after the 1981–1982 season, it meant the end of the final rounds in Pittsburgh.

Nicknamed the "Senator," Pete Strickland came to Pittsburgh from the successful basketball program at DeMatha Catholic High School in Washington, D.C. He played his high school ball for the legendary coach Morgan Wooten. Extroverted and personable, Strickland was a theater arts major at Pitt and a fine point guard for the Panthers (1975–1979). He led the team in assists for three straight seasons. Strickland later became the head basketball coach at Coastal Carolina University.

Point guard Dwayne Wallace was a four-year letter winner (1979–1982) from Baltimore, Maryland. Recruited by Tim Grgurich, Wallace came on strong during his last two seasons under new coach Roy Chipman, directing the Panthers to back-to-back Eastern Eight Tournament championships and NCAA appearances. He led the Panthers in assists for three consecutive seasons and also was tops on the team in steals as a senior (1981–1982). Wallace was named to the Eastern Eight's All-Tournament Team for his play against Rutgers University and West Virginia University in 1982.

Four

MOVING UP TO
THE BIG EAST

Big East Conference Commissioner Dave Gavitt predicted that it was only a matter of time until getting a ticket to a Pitt basketball game in Pittsburgh would be the one of the toughest sports challenges. He was right. In their first season (1982–1983) of Big East competition, the Panthers attracted large crowds for conference games. In a space of 19 days in February, Pitt defeated three nationally ranked Big East opponents: Saint John's (72-71), Syracuse (85-74), and Georgetown (65-63). Saint John's featured Chris Mullin, and Georgetown had star center Patrick Ewing. (Photograph by Michael F. Fabus.)

Dave Gavitt (center), the one-time Providence College coach, came to Pittsburgh in the fall of 1981 as commissioner of the Big East Conference. He extended the official invitation to the University of Pittsburgh to join the Big East in 1982–1983. Welcoming Gavitt to the Pitt campus are Pitt's director of athletics Cas Myslinski (left) and basketball coach Roy Chipman (right). Pitt had been a member of the Eastern Athletic Association (Eastern Eight) since its inception in 1976.

One of coach Roy Chipman's first recruits to Pittsburgh was a stocky six-foot, five-inch forward from Mount Vernon, New York. Clyde Vaughan was a prime player in the Panthers' move from the Eastern Eight to the Big East. As it turned out, he played a starring role in both leagues. Vaughan helped lead the Panthers to a pair of NCAA Tournament appearances in his first two seasons and was named the Most Outstanding Player of the 1982 Eastern Eight Tournament. A tremendous shooter and strong rebounder, Vaughan was an All-Big East selection during his junior and senior seasons. (Photograph by George Gojkovich.)

Dr. Roy Chipman was named Pitt's 10th head basketball coach at a press conference in the spring of 1980. Chipman came to Pitt following a successful stint as head coach at Lafayette College, a school in the eastern part of Pennsylvania. He took the Panthers to the NCAA Tournament in each of his first two seasons (1980–1982).

Followers of Pittsburgh-area high school basketball were familiar with Baldwin High School's 6-foot, 11-inch center Ed Scheuermann. Scheuermann turned down scholarship offers from several high-profile programs to attend Pitt, where he was a four-time letterman (1976–1981). Injuries hampered Scheuermann throughout his career, but he did have one particularly memorable game, a 23-point, 14-rebound effort in the Panthers' 89-86 overtime win against Lefty Driesell's University of Maryland Terrapins at the Civic Arena on February 11, 1978.

Roosevelt "Boo" Kirby was a junior college transfer forward who played only one season (1981–1982) at Pitt, but it was a productive one. A forward, Kirby, and Clyde Vaughan, right, helped shoulder most of the inside burden for the 1981–1982 Panthers. In this photograph, Kirby waits for a rebound in Pitt's win against West Virginia University in the 1982 Eastern Eight Tournament championship game at Pittsburgh's Civic Arena.

Assistant coach Seth Greenberg demonstrates technique for the benefit of guard George Allen. Greenberg and Allen were both New Yorkers; Greenberg hailed from Long Island and Allen from New York City. Greenberg later became a head coach, first at Long Beach State University and then at the University of South Florida. His 2001–2002 University of South Florida team was one of only five teams to defeat the Panthers in 2001–2002. The Bulls beat Pitt in the finals of the University Hoops Classic at Robert Morris College on Thanksgiving weekend.

Roy Chipman directed Pitt to the Eastern Eight Tournament championship during his first season (1980–1981) and then came back and did the same in 1981–1982. The second victory, in Pitt's final season in the Eastern Eight Conference, was particularly sweet. In this photograph, Chipman celebrates the Panthers' 79-72 victory against West Virginia University in the finals of the 1982 tournament. West Virginia had entered the game with a record of 26-2, including a pair of victories against Pitt during the regular season. The second game, an 82-77 West Virginia win before a WVU Coliseum record crowd of 16,704, ran the Mountaineers' winning streak to 24 games. After the game, when discussing whether Pitt and West Virginia would continue to play twice a season because of Pitt's move to the Big East, West Virginia coach Gale Catlett referred to Pitt's program as "mediocre." Chipman looked forward to a possible third meeting against West Virginia. "I'm not saying we will beat them," Chipman said, "but I know we can beat them." Behind the inspired play of Clyde Vaughan and point guard Dwayne Wallace, the Panthers rolled to victory before a fired-up, sold-out Civic Arena crowd, split almost down the middle between Pitt and West Virginia fans. It was the Panthers' final Eastern Eight game. "Maybe they'll invite us back," Chipman quipped after the game.

A rarity in Pittsburgh college basketball circles, Darryl Shepherd played for both Pitt and Duquesne University during his collegiate career. He enrolled at Duquesne for his freshman season (1981–1982), but transferred to Pitt after one year, where he was a member of some of Roy Chipman's earliest Big East teams. A tremendous leaper with good quickness, Shepherd played in three postseason tournaments during his days with the Panthers.

Shepherd, who also ran track during his college years at Pitt, was a self-taught musician who learned to play several musical instruments while in high school. He later went on to produce rhythm-and-blues records. He was confident about his chances early on in the business. "Most of the big record producers know who I am," he once told a Pittsburgh writer.

Clyde Vaughan led the Panthers in scoring and rebounding for three consecutive seasons (1981–1984). As a sophomore in 1981–1982, Pitt's final season in the Big East, he led the conference in scoring and was second in rebounding, but was snubbed by the league's head coaches; he failed to make either of the Eastern Eight's first two All-Conference teams. Vaughan did earn All-Tournament and Outstanding Player honors for his play in the league's tournament, but that was voted on by media representatives, and it was after the regular season. Pitt officials decided to turn the snub into a positive and took advantage of this unique photograph opportunity to pose Vaughan with actor and comedian Rodney Dangerfield, a man who has made a living on the premise that he does not get any respect, when Dangerfield happened to be in Pittsburgh one day in 1982. Vaughan had a distinguished career in Pittsburgh and was the 1984 recipient of Pitt's prestigious Blue-Gold Award. His name is etched in stone along the Varsity Walk, the sidewalk between the Cathedral of Learning and Heinz Chapel on the Pitt campus. After playing professionally in Europe for a number of years, Vaughan entered the coaching ranks and was most recently an assistant coach at the University of South Florida.

Charles Smith remains one of the greatest—and most important—players in Pitt's basketball history. When Pitt joined the Big East in 1982, it expanded its recruiting scope far beyond anything it had ever been. Pitt could now go after prominent players from distant parts of the country and succeed in drawing them to Pittsburgh. Smith, who had been a high school All-American in Bridgeport, Connecticut, is the all-time leading scorer (2,045 points) in school history. He was Big East Freshman of the Year in 1984–1985.

Charles Smith gave the Panthers a dominant, intimidating presence in the middle. In this photograph, he blocks a shot in the Panthers' 102-77 win against Duquesne University at the Civic Arena on January 12, 1987. Pat Cavanaugh (beneath Smith) rushes in to assist. The Panthers dominated their city rival throughout the 1980s, winning nine straight from 1982 to 1988. Smith was named Big East Player of the Year in 1987–1988 and had legions of admirers. "If there's a better center in the country, I haven't seen him," said Providence College coach Rick Pitino.

Head coach Roy Chipman prepares to plot strategy with two of his most prominent recruits at Pitt, Curtis Aiken (No. 14) and Jerome Lane (No. 34). The Big East Conference's television exposure and national reputation enhanced the reputations of all its members, and Chipman and his staff were able to bring several highly touted recruits to Pittsburgh. Aiken was a shooting guard from Buffalo, New York, who went on to score 1,200 points from 1983 to 1987. He led the Panthers in both steals and assists in 1984–1985. Lane was a physical power forward whose primary forte was rebounding, yet he could do just about anything else on a basketball court. He was a two-time All-American and All-Big East selection who could be simply overpowering inside. "Lane is a glass eater who dominates the boards like no one in the country," observed ESPN's Dick Vitale.

Before the Big East Conference, Pitt would play an occasional home game at the Civic Arena downtown. The Panthers met Notre Dame at the arena in back-to-back seasons during the mid-1970s and also played Maryland there in 1978. Pitt's usual Civic Arena dates involved Duquesne University, either as an opponent or as a co-host for an in-season tournament. There was the Steel Bowl for many years, followed by the ill-fated Golden Triangle Classic. In 1976, Pitt and Duquesne invited the University of Pennsylvania and Penn State University to the Civic Arena for a pair of Friday-Saturday doubleheaders during the last weekend in January. But, when Pitt basketball tickets became treasured finds toward the late 1980s, Pitt moved its annual Big East games with Georgetown and Syracuse to the more spacious Civic Arena. The Panthers also played North Carolina, Arizona, Georgia, Villanova, Connecticut, Saint John's, and UCLA at the downtown facility, which is also home to the National Hockey League's Pittsburgh Penguins. (Photograph by Michael F. Fabus.)

Paul Evans developed a national reputation for winning basketball when he coached David Robinson at the U.S. Naval Academy during the mid-1980s. Pitt officials hired him away from Navy after the 1985–1986 season. Evans's tenure (1986–1994) at Pitt remains one of the most successful—and gut wrenching—in the school's basketball history. Like Chipman before him, Evans led his first two Pitt teams (1986–1988) to NCAA Tournament appearances, but both ended with disappointing losses in the second round. In all, Evans's Pitt teams played in five NCAA Tournaments, more than any coach in school history. Only Doc Carlson (367) and Bob Timmons (174) won more games as coach of the Panthers, and both spent considerably longer terms in Pittsburgh. Evans, who averaged 20 wins per season, helped direct the Panthers to new heights, including a No. 2 national ranking at one point of the 1987–1988 season. His 1987–1988 Panthers won the school's first outright Big East regular-season championship. His Pitt teams defeated every team in the Big East, plus non-conference foes the University of Arizona, UCLA, the University of Kansas, and the University of Kentucky. Evans was dismissed following a 13-14 season in 1993–1994.

A husky forward with soft hands and a wonderful shooting touch, Rod Brookin captivated Panther fans with his unique scoring style from 1987 to 1990. Brookin was recruited to Pittsburgh from Steelton-Highspire High School, a school with a traditionally strong basketball program in the eastern part of Pennsylvania. At Pitt, Brookin contributed to three consecutive postseason tournament teams. He finished his playing career with 1,047 points. Brookin later went into coaching basketball.

Head coach Paul Evans (kneeling) directs the Panthers during his early years as Pitt's coach. On the bench, from left to right, are longtime Evans aides Norm Law and Mark Coleman. To the right of Evans, with his left hand on his mouth, is John Calipari, who later was head coach at the University of Massachusetts and of the NBA's New Jersey Nets before returning to the college ranks as head coach at the University of Memphis. The Pitt player at the far right is Demetreus Gore. (Photograph by Mike Drazdzinski.)

Pitt All-American Charles Smith pulls in this rebound in front of Syracuse University's Rony Seikaly in this photograph from Pitt's 63-61 win against the Orangemen at the Civic Arena on February 9, 1987. The Panthers defeated Syracuse twice during the regular season that year, but the Orangemen came back to beat Pitt in the semifinals of the Big East Tournament at Madison Square Garden in New York City.

Jerome Lane is doing what he did best—rebound—in the first round of the Pitt-University of Kansas game during the 1986 Rainbow Classic in Hawaii. The Panthers defeated the Jayhawks 79-76 and went on to beat the University of Arkansas and the University of Wisconsin to claim the holiday tournament championship. This was the first season for new coach Paul Evans.

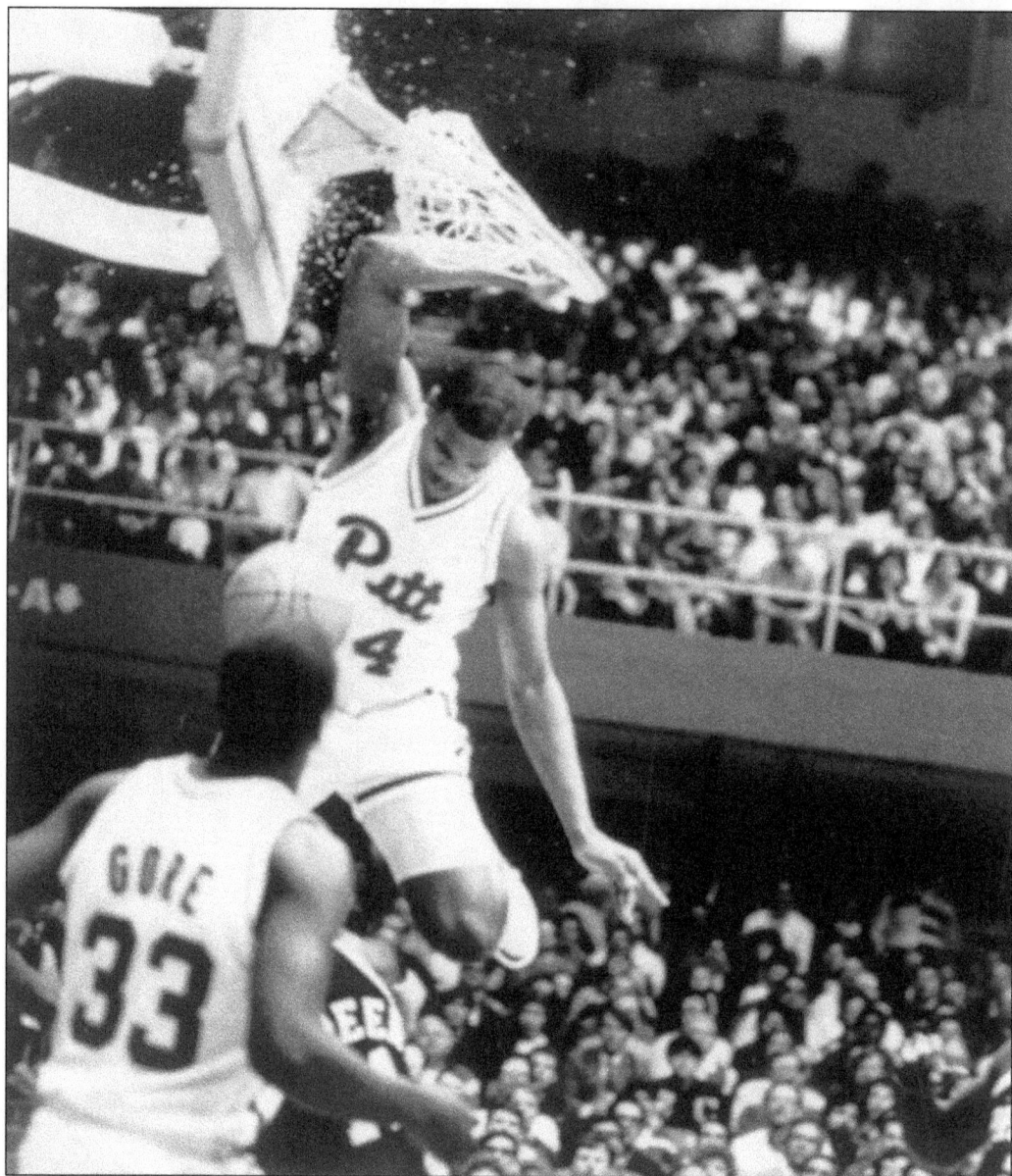

On January 25, 1988, Jerome Lane gave Pitt fans a wondrous thrill when his tomahawk dunk against Providence College bent the rim and shattered the backboard at Fitzgerald Field House. With 16 minutes, 36 seconds remaining in the first half, Lane took a pass from point guard Sean Miller, and the rest is visual history. The incident caused a 30-minute delay in the game. Pitt went on to defeat the Friars 90-56 on its way to the 1987–1988 Big East regular-season championship. The *Pittsburgh Post-Gazette* later named Lane's smashing dunk the No. 1 Pitt basketball moment in the history of Fitzgerald Field House. Lane ranks among Pitt's all-time leading scorers and rebounders. "No one in the country, I don't care how big he is, can out-rebound Jerome Lane one-on-one," was the way Syracuse University coach Jim Boeheim described Lane following his 29-point, 15-rebound game in a win at Syracuse on March 6, 1988. That victory, in the last game of the regular season, gave the Panthers the Big East title. (Photograph by Mike Drazdzinski.)

Point guard Sean Miller, right, and shooting guard Jason Matthews were both freshman members of Pitt's heralded recruiting class of 1987. Also included in that group were Brian Shorter, Bobby Martin, and Darelle Porter. The 1987–1988 season also happened to be the University of Pittsburgh's Bicentennial (note the special patch on Miller's left sleeve). Miller started for the Panthers as a freshman and helped lead the team to the Big East regular-season title in his first season of collegiate competition. He was named Big East Freshman of the Year. Miller was from Beaver Falls, Pennsylvania. Matthews took a longer route to college; he was recruited to Pitt from Los Angeles, California. He received All-Big East honors in each of his four seasons. Both Miller and Matthews were exceptional shooters and rank among the Big East Conference all-time leaders in free throw percentage. Both scored more than 1,000 points in their college careers. Matthews continues to reside and work in Pittsburgh. Miller went into coaching and has worked as an assistant coach at the University of Wisconsin, Pitt, North Carolina State University, and Xavier University.

Brian Shorter lays in two of his 37 points during the Panthers' thrilling 99-91 win against third-ranked Oklahoma on January 15, 1989, at Fitzgerald Field House. "That's the player I recruited," Pitt coach Paul Evans told reporters afterward. "He needs to dominate all games like he did today." Said Shorter, "They [Oklahoma] weren't contesting many of my shots. They were just standing there, and I shot over them."

Bobby Martin (No. 55) and Brian Shorter complemented each other well during their respective careers (1987–1991). Recruited to Pitt from Atlantic City, New Jersey, Martin was a talented, consistent performer throughout his career. As a freshman, he calmly sank a pair of free throws to ice a Pitt win at West Virginia University (the Panthers' only win in Morgantown during the 1980s). In his junior season, Martin had a brilliant 27-point, 20-rebound performance on the road against Georgetown University. (Photograph by Michael F. Fabus.)

Though perhaps not remembered with the same tone of reverence as teammates Curtis Aiken, Jerome Lane, and Charles Smith, Demetreus Gore was a major factor in a lot of wins for the University of Pittsburgh basketball program during the 1980s. Nicknamed "Freakazoid," Gore was from Detroit, Michigan. He brought a myriad of talents to Pittsburgh but is most commonly known for his scoring ability on a basketball court. Gore lettered four times under coaches Roy Chipman and Paul Evans and finished his career with 1,563 points. He was a third-team All-Big East selection in 1985–1986. He also led the Panthers in steals that season. The Panthers participated in four postseason tournaments—three NCAA Tournaments and one NIT—during Gore's career (1984–1988). (Photograph by George Gojkovich.)

Pitt's Brock Generalovich, the son of former Panther star Brian Generalovich, walked on to the Pitt basketball team and ultimately lettered for the Panthers of Paul Evans in the late 1980s and early 1990s. In this photograph from December 16, 1989, Generalovich drives against Robert Morris College's (now Robert Morris University) Brett Vincent. The Panthers won this game 88-71 at Fitzgerald Field House. Robert Morris has never defeated Pitt in basketball, nor has any team from the Northeast Conference for that matter. Vincent is an interesting story in his own way, in relation to Pitt basketball trivia. His father, Don Vincent, captained West Virginia University's team that finished the 1957–1958 season with a record of 26-2. Brett Vincent holds the unique distinction of having represented three different schools—West Virginia, Robert Morris, and Marshall University—as a player against the University of Pittsburgh. He originally enrolled at West Virginia, transferred to Robert Morris, and then transferred again to Marshall and played for each in one game against Pitt. (Photograph by Chaz Palla.)

Tim Glover was a native of Texas who played only his freshman season (1990–1991) for the Panthers, but his crowning moment came during that lone campaign when he came off the bench to spark Pitt with his three-point shooting ability in an NCAA Tournament first-round game in Louisville, Kentucky. The Panthers defeated the University of Georgia in overtime 76-68 before being eliminated in the next round by the University of Kansas. This photograph was from the Pitt-Georgia game. (Photograph by Paul Diamond.)

Sean Miller misfired on this last-second, three-point shot attempt versus the University of Florida in a second-round NIT game at Fitzgerald Field House on March 23, 1992. Miller continues to be a familiar name in western Pennsylvania basketball. Late-night television watchers first caught his basketball act when, as a youth, he appeared on the *Tonight Show* with Johnny Carson, demonstrating his ball-handling skills and tricks. Miller also produced an instructional basketball video with the help of his father, John Miller, who was his coach at Blackhawk High School. (Photograph by Harry Bloomberg.)

Later in this ballgame, Pitt's Garrick Thomas (No. 4) nailed a three-point basket from the top of the key to give the Panthers a stunning 76-73 victory against seventh-ranked Seton Hall University, coached at the time by P.J. Carlesimo. The date was January 16, 1993, and a full house was on hand at Fitzgerald Field House for the exciting Saturday night thriller. Thomas finished the game with 19 points for the Panthers, who ended the season with an NCAA first-round loss to the University of Utah. It was Pitt's last NCAA appearance before the 2001–2002 season. At halftime of this Pitt-Seton Hall game, incoming football coach John Majors, who had also coached the Panthers from 1973 to 1976, was introduced to the crowd during a special halftime ceremony. (Photograph by Harry Bloomberg.)

Orlando Antigua overcame an impoverished childhood and adolescence in his native New York City to become one of the most inspirational stories in the history of Pitt's basketball program. The innocent victim of a street shooting during his sophomore year in high school, Antigua and his family were homeless two years later. Antigua persevered, earned a scholarship to Pitt, graduated, and played excellent basketball for the Panthers. He was named to the Big East's All-Rookie Team in 1991–1992 and in 1994 was the recipient of the U.S. Basketball Writers Association's Most Courageous Athlete Award. (Photograph by Harry Bloomberg.)

When his fine playing career at Pitt ended, Orlando Antigua became the first Hispanic member of the world-famous Harlem Globetrotters. He spent six years with the Globetrotters before retiring from active basketball in 2002. He went to work for another former Pitt basketball player, Pat Cavanaugh, who owns and operates a successful marketing firm in Pittsburgh. Antigua's younger brother, Oliver Antigua, spent a short time as an assistant coach at Pitt under Ralph Willard.

101

A bruising 6-foot, 10-inch center, Darren Morningstar preferred wearing his sideburns long, but he was all business on the basketball court. A transfer from the U.S. Naval Academy, Morningstar's playing style typified the type of inside game Paul Evans liked—big, strong, and physical. Panther fans will never forget Morningstar's 27-point, 10-rebound game in the Panthers' surprising 85-67 defeat of Kentucky at Rupp Arena in 1991. (Photograph by Chaz Palla.)

Darelle Porter was an outstanding scholastic football and basketball player at Pittsburgh's Perry Traditional Academy. A receiver in football, he accepted a basketball scholarship to Pitt and did everything well during his four seasons (1987–1991) as a Panther. He led the team in steals and assists in two different seasons and ranks second, behind Sean Miller, on the Panthers' all-time assists list. Porter spent three seasons (1998–2001) as head basketball coach at Duquesne University. (Photograph by Chaz Palla.)

Pitt center Eric Mobley (No. 52) was a big man at 6-feet, 11-inches, but even he came up a little bit short when standing next to UCLA's 7-foot, 245-pound George Zidek. UCLA paid a visit to Pittsburgh to face the Panthers on December 28, 1992. It was the Bruins' first appearance in Pittsburgh since the 1970 Steel Bowl. This time the Panthers were victorious, outlasting UCLA 91-79. It was one of five games the Panthers played at the Civic Arena during the 1992–1993 season. Pitt was 2-3 in those games. Mobley was a good-natured man from New York City who joined fellow New York City recruits Jerry McCullough and Orlando Antigua in the Steel City. Mobley lettered three times (1992–1994) and was taken in the first round of the 1994 NBA draft by the Milwaukee Bucks. (Photograph by Harry Bloomberg.)

Ralph Willard's five-year run (1994–1999) was not nearly as successful as the Paul Evans era, but it did have its moments of excitement. Unfortunately for Willard and the Pitt basketball program, too much of the news had to do with injuries, ineligibilities, suspensions, and legal problems. On February 1, 1999, Willard announced that he would be stepping down at the conclusion of the season. Willard was a hot commodity when he was introduced as Pitt's new coach in 1994. His previous team, Western Kentucky, had made waves in the NCAA; the Hilltoppers had upset Big East heavyweight Seton Hall in the 1993 tournament. Providence College had also tried to lure Willard, but he accepted the job in Pittsburgh. His tenure was highlighted by two wins against Saint John's in his first season, and an upset of Kentucky at the San Juan Shootout in Puerto Rico the day after Thanksgiving in 1998. After leaving Pitt, Willard became the head coach at his alma mater, Holy Cross, and guided the Crusaders to the NCAA Tournament in 2001 and 2002. (Photograph by Harry Bloomberg.)

Chad Varga was one of Ralph Willard's first Pitt recruits—a junior college transfer who played very well for Willard's first three Pitt teams (1994-97). A strong 6-6 forward, he was a solid scorer, rebounder and leader. As a senior, Varga helped lead the Panthers to the NIT, where they defeated the University of New Orleans in the opening round before losing at the University of Arkansas in the second round of play. Varga led the 1995–1996 Panthers in rebounding. (Photograph by Harry Bloomberg.)

It was a family affair for Ralph Willard at Pitt. His son, Kevin Willard, was a backup point guard for the Panthers from 1996 to 1997. The Willards are the only father-son coach-player combination in Pitt basketball history. The younger Willard originally enrolled at Western Kentucky, where his father was head coach at the time, but decided to come to Pittsburgh too. Kevin Willard gave up a final year of eligibility to accept a position with Rick Pitino and the Boston Celtics.

Pitt center Mark Blount (center) and teammates Jason Maile (No. 22) and Vonteego Cummings (No. 3) appear to be in perfect position for a missed shot during this Pitt-Seton Hall game at Fitzgerald Field House. Blount played just two seasons (1995–1997) at Pitt before declaring himself eligible for the NBA draft. He was taken by the Seattle Supersonics in the second round in 1997. He finally made it with an NBA team when he latched on with the Boston Celtics in 2001. Blount was Pitt's leading rebounder as a sophomore. (Photograph by Image Point Pittsburgh.)

Kellii Taylor (1997–1999) was one of Ralph Willard's earliest recruits. He had amazing hands and quickness and excelled on defense. He was also especially good in the open court on a fast break. Taylor led the Panthers in steals in two different seasons and established a school single-season mark for thefts (101) during the 1996–1997 season. On two different occasions, Taylor was credited with seven steals in one game. (Photograph by Sean Brady.)

One of the most graceful and exciting players ever to wear a Pitt basketball uniform, guard Vonteego Cummings was a prize recruit for Ralph Willard. Cummings was from Thomson, Georgia, and showed his prowess right from the start, leading the Panthers in scoring in a win against Duquesne University in his first collegiate game. Cummings thrilled Panther fans with breathtaking drives to the basket, his dazzling one-on-one moves, and his impressive assortment of dunks. Cummings was a three-time All-Big East Conference selection. Another career 1,000-point scorer, he was a catalyst in the Panthers' late-season drive to the NIT in 1997. He scored the game-winning basket in the final seconds of the Panthers' Big East Tournament game victory against the University of Connecticut in 1997. The following year, he scored 37 points in a first-round Big East Tournament loss to Villanova University. Following his college career, Cummings played two seasons with the NBA's Golden State Warriors before being traded to the Philadelphia 76ers. (Photograph by Image Point Pittsburgh.)

Steady, mature Gerald Jordan had a calming influence over the rest of his teammates during his two seasons (1995–1997) with the Panthers. He helped lead a late-season surge as a senior (1996–1997) that saw the Panthers receive an NIT invitation. The Panthers finished Jordan's senior year with an 18-15 record, including a 10-8 mark in Big East play. It was the only winning season during Ralph Willard's coaching tenure at Pitt. (Photograph by Harry Bloomberg.)

Vonteego Cummings was not a natural point guard, but injuries and other circumstances dictated that he move to that position later in his collegiate career. Cummings never complained and was a model of consistency for four consecutive seasons. He led the Panthers in scoring for three straight seasons and is one of only two Panthers to finish their careers among the school's top 10 in scoring, assists, and steals. Ricardo Greer is the other. (Photograph by Harry Bloomberg.)

Jason Maile was one of the Panthers' top three-point shooters during his career (1992–1997). On February 12, 1997, the fifth-year senior scored 40 points—including all eight of his shot attempts in the second half—to push the Panthers to a 95-89 win against Villanova University at Fitzgerald Field House. In 1994–1995, Maile led the Panthers in three-point shooting percentage (40.8) and led the team in free throw percentage in two seasons. (Photograph by Harry Bloomberg.)

Jarrett Lockhart was a fine shooting guard who played his first three seasons (1997–2000) for Ralph Willard and his senior year under a new coach, Ben Howland. Lockhart was from New York City and was the Panthers' top three-point shooter during the late 1990s. He made exactly 61 treys in two different seasons (1997–1998 and 1999–2000). He had the team's best three-point field goal percentage (38.1) during his sophomore season. (Photograph by Harry Bloomberg.)

A couple of Pittsburgh kids, Bill Hillgrove, left, and Dick Groat have been calling all the Pitt basketball action together since 1979–1980. Hillgrove, a graduate of Duquesne University, began as Pitt's football play-by-play man in 1974 and still does Panthers football. He became the radio voice of the Pittsburgh Steelers in 1994. Groat, the College Basketball Player of the Year in 1952 at Duke University, played in the NBA and with the baseball Pittsburgh Pirates. In 1960, Groat was the National League's batting champion and Most Valuable Player. The Pirates defeated the New York Yankees in a thrilling seven-game World Series that year.

This photograph was taken at Fitzgerald Field House on January 23, 1999. The occasion was the celebration of the 25th anniversary of the University of Pittsburgh's 25-4 basketball season of 1973–1974. From left to right are assistant coach Fran Webster, Betty Ridl (wife of the team's late head coach, Buzz Ridl), Billy Knight, and Mickey Martin.

Ben Howland met the Pittsburgh-area press for the first time when he was introduced as the University of Pittsburgh's new head basketball coach during a March 1999 press conference at Pitt Stadium. Howland accepted the Pitt job following a five-year stint at Northern Arizona University, where he took the Lumberjacks to the school's first-ever NCAA Tournament appearance in 1998. Howland talked about his basketball philosophy during that first press conference, stressing the need to "recruit to shoot." His teams at Northern Arizona had been some of the nation's best in shooting the ball, and he hoped to do the same for Pittsburgh. (Photograph by Charles LeClaire.)

This photograph was taken prior to the Pitt-Rutgers University game at Fitzgerald Field House on February 25, 2001. The ceremony honored Rutgers's Jeff Greer, far left, and his brother, Pitt's Ricardo Greer, far right. The Greers had become the Big East's all-time leading scorers for brothers that season. Also taking part in the ceremony were, from left to right, Rutgers coach Kevin Bannon, Pitt's director of athletics Steve Pederson, and Pitt coach Ben Howland.

Nobody gave the Panthers much of a chance at the 2001 Big East Tournament in New York City, but senior Ricardo Greer played like a man possessed, leading Pitt to victories against the University of Miami, the University of Notre Dame, and Syracuse University on successive nights. The Panthers finally lost to Boston College in the championship game, but Pitt used the late-season push as its battle cry "Remember the Run" heading into the 2001–2002 season. (Photograph by Sean Brady.)

University of Pittsburgh chancellor Mark Nordenberg, far right, and director of athletics Steve Pederson, far left, welcome John and Gertrude Petersen to the Pitt campus. The Petersens donated $10 million toward costs for the new basketball arena/convocation center built on the former site of Pitt Stadium. The gift was the largest individual contribution in Pitt's history. "The University of Pittsburgh is on the move, and the Petersens have given our efforts a huge boost by making such a sizeable and well-targeted investment in our future," said Nordenberg.

Five

IT WAS A
VERY GOOD YEAR

University of Pittsburgh players, coaches, and support personnel had every reason to smile for this March 2, 2002 photograph. The Panthers had just defeated West Virginia University 92-65 at Fitzgerald Field House in the final regular season game of the 2001–2002 season. The Panthers proudly display the trophy, symbolizing their Big East Conference West Division title.

During the 2001–2002 season, Brandin Knight became a household name in college basketball circles. The junior guard enjoyed a marvelous season, leading the Panthers to the Sweet Sixteen of the NCAA Tournament. Knight grew up in a basketball family; his father, Mel Knight, coached for many years at the junior college level in New Jersey, and Brandin's older brother, Brevin Knight, is a veteran NBA player.

From 1925 to 1999, Pittsburgh sports fans flocked up "Cardiac Hill" in Oakland to watch football games and other events at Pitt Stadium. The familiar view up DeSoto Street changed forever when Pitt Stadium was demolished in early 2000. This 2001 photograph shows construction of the new Petersen Events Center. The extended area of the building, seen here, is designed to be the main entrance area of the facility. (Photograph by Sean Brady.)

Delirious Pitt students celebrate following the Panthers' 72-57 victory against 10th-ranked Syracuse University on January 22, 2002, at Fitzgerald Field House. It was Pitt's first win against the Orangemen at Fitzgerald since the 1982–1983 season, Pitt's first year in Big East competition. The sellout crowd of 6,798 started a string of six consecutive full houses for Panther games at Pitt's Field House. (Photograph by Sean Brady.)

This 2002 photograph shows continued progress of the construction of the new Petersen Events Center on the University of Pittsburgh campus. University officials directed a guided media tour of the building on January 10, 2002. Director of athletics Steve Pederson announced that day that Pitt officials had been hoping that Pitt's commencement activities in late April 2002 could be held at the Petersen Center, but the new facility was not quite ready. Commencement was held at Mellon Arena in downtown Pittsburgh. (Photograph by Sean Brady.)

A high-flying guard from Buffalo, New York, Julius Page was an early Ben Howland recruit to Pittsburgh. He played a key role in the Panthers' run to the finals of the Big East Tournament in 2000–2001 and then came back and had a solid sophomore season, teaming with point guard Brandin Knight to give the Panthers a dynamite backcourt both offensively and defensively. (Photograph by William McBride.)

Born in Klaipeda, Lithuania, Donatas Zavackas moved to the United States and played his high school basketball in New Jersey. He spent his senior year at St. Vincent-St. Mary in Ohio, but did not play ball because of Ohio high school transfer rules. He became a starter for the Panthers in 2000–2001 and stepped up his production even more the following season. Zavackas is one of the team's top three-point shooters. (Photograph by Harry Bloomberg.)

The "first family" of University of Pittsburgh basketball, shown during the summer before the 2001–2002 season, includes head coach Ben Howland, his wife, Kim, daughter, Meredith, and son, Adam. "He is as fine a family man as I've ever known, and it is an honor and a privilege to be his friend," University of Utah coach Rick Majerus said about Howland.

Sophomore center Toree Morris delivers two points the easy way during Pitt's 72-57 Big East victory against Syracuse University at Fitzgerald Field House. Morris contributed eight points and seven rebounds that night for the Panthers, who later beat the Orangemen for a second time at the Carrier Dome in Syracuse. That victory gave the Panthers three consecutive wins against Syracuse. (Photograph by Harry Bloomberg.)

Chevon Troutman was named "Mr. Pennsylvania Basketball 2000" by pasportsfever.com in a poll of fans, media, and coaches. He sat out his freshman season (2000–2001) at Pitt and played little during the first half of the 2001–2002 campaign. He started for the Panthers in early-season wins against Morgan State University and Northern Arizona University but did not see significant action until the final six or seven weeks of the season. He started the Panthers' last two games: NCAA meetings against the University of California and Kent State University. (Photograph by Harry Bloomberg.)

Ontario Lett was a late addition to the 2001–2002 Pitt basketball roster, but he turned out to be a major contributor to the team's amazing 29-6 season. A junior college transfer from Pensacola, Florida, Lett provided the Panthers with some important bulk and muscle inside. A smart player with good hands, instincts, and nice offensive moves, Lett helped negate the departures of seniors Ricardo Greer and Isaac Hawkins from the previous year's team.

This photograph from inside Fitzgerald Field House was snapped while the ball was in the air to start the last-ever college basketball game at the 50-year-old building. West Virginia University provided the opposition this night. The Mountaineers kept the game close during the first half, but the Panthers pulled away for a relatively easy win.

Many outstanding former players from Pitt's basketball history returned to campus the first weekend in March 2002 to celebrate the program's tradition and the last college basketball game at Fitzgerald Field House. Players from all decades were in attendance, including one of the greatest names in Pitt basketball annals, Charles Smith. Smith, seen here with his children, took a walk across the Fitzgerald Field House court as part of a special halftime ceremony.

119

The Fitzgerald Field House scoreboard tells the story as it ticks its final second of action on March 2, 2002. The Panthers defeated West Virginia University 92-65. Panther guards Julius Page (No. 1) and Brandin Knight (No. 20) head out to the court to greet the rest of their victorious teammates, including freshman Yuri Demetris (arm raised). The Fitzgerald Field House floor was cleared following the game for a number of special presentations. Big East Conference commissioner Michael Tranghese presented the team with its 2001–2002 Big East Conference West Division trophy, and Pitt officials raised a banner in honor of the accomplishment. The last college basketball game at Fitzgerald Field House was not the last basketball game played there. High school tournament and all-star games will continue to be played at Fitzgerald, continuing a longstanding Pittsburgh tradition. Pitt's wrestling, volleyball, and gymnastics teams also plan to use Fitzgerald Field House for their home contests in the years ahead. (Photograph by Image Point Pittsburgh.)

Ontario Lett hoists the trophy symbolic of the Panthers' 2001–2002 Big East Conference West Division title. The Panthers actually clinched the regular-season championship on February 26, 2002, when they beat Seton Hall University 73-66 in overtime, but the official presentation to the team was delayed until after the final home game of the season. Jaron Brown (No. 4) is on the far left, Brandin Knight has his right hand on Lett's front, and Chad Johnson (wearing a headband), the only senior on the team, appears on the far right.

With a 2001-2002 Big East trophy shining in the background, Pitt head coach Ben Howland addressed the crowd at Fitzgerald Field House following the final game of the regular season. Few people had left Fitzgerald Field House after its final game. Many spectators mingled with friends, and cameras clicked away, recording the moment. Howland was particularly busy in the next month, picking up a few trophies for his own collection.

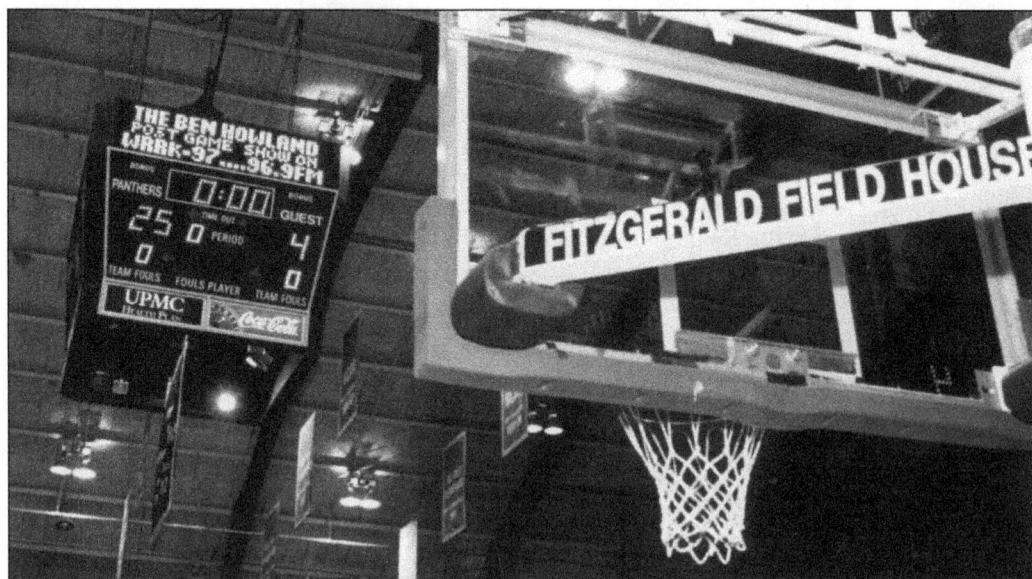

The Fitzgerald Field House scoreboard tells the story of the Panthers' wonderful final season in the old building. Pitt finished the regular season with a record of 25-4, tying (at the time) the school record set by the 1973–1974 Panthers for victories in one season. (Photograph by Image Point Pittsburgh.)

Trainer Tony Salesi (far right) tends to the sore right knees of starting guards Brandin Knight (left) and Julius Page (center). This moment came late in the final game at Fitzgerald Field House on March 2, 2002. The injuries were not serious, and both men were healthy and ready to go for both the Big East and NCAA Tournaments. (Photograph by Image Point Pittsburgh.)

Mark McCaroll (left) and Ontario Lett start the celebration during the final moments of Pitt's 63-50 victory against the University of California in the second round of the 2002 NCAA Tournament. The game was played at Mellon Arena—formerly the Civic Arena—in Pittsburgh. The arena had also hosted first- and second-round games of March Madness in 1997. Duquesne University was host school for both events. This photograph was taken on Sunday, March 17, 2002. It was the second game of an NCAA doubleheader. UCLA had upset Cincinnati in double overtime in the first game, a fact that seemed to make a lot of Pittsburgh fans happy. The majority of the crowd rooted for UCLA against the favored Bearcats. Note the Pitt fans behind the bench cheering as the Pitt-California game drew to its conclusion. The victory advanced the Panthers to the Sweet Sixteen, where their storybook season ended with a loss to Kent State University at Rupp Arena in Lexington, Kentucky. (Photograph by Mike Drazdzinski.)

Brandin Knight suffered a knee injury during the final seconds of the Big East Tournament Championship on March 9 and spent the next few days assuring the media that he would be playing in the NCAA Tournament. "My leg is fine," Knight said. "This is one of the reasons I came to Pittsburgh, to play in the tournament. So please, no more questions about the knee." In this photograph, Knight shoots for two in the Panthers' NCAA victory against the University of California on March 17 in Pittsburgh. (Photograph by Mike Drazdzinski.)

Head coach Ben Howland (left) and point guard Brandin Knight receive their Big East Conference awards during a special banquet the night before the start of the 2002 Big East Tournament at Madison Square Garden in New York City. This photograph was taken on March 5, 2002. Howland was named the 2001–2002 Big East Coach of the Year, and Knight shared Co-Player of the Year honors with the University of Connecticut's Caron Butler. (Photograph by Tom Maguire.)

This panoramic photograph from March 15, 2002, shows Pittsburgh's Mellon Arena during the late stages of Pitt's opening-round victory against Central Connecticut State University. With the NCAA Tournament Selection Committee making a concentrated effort to keep higher-seeded teams closer to home for their first two games, the fact that the Panthers played in Pittsburgh was no great surprise. (Photograph by Mike Drazdzinski.)

NCAA "Selection Sunday" has become one of the most anticipated days on the college basketball calendar. Teams often convene to watch the Sunday spectacle, and the 2001–2002 Panthers were no exception. They gathered inside the William Pitt Union on Pitt's campus to find out what their plans would be for the opening rounds. In this March 10, 2002 photograph, Julius Page answers questions from local media representatives.

A preseason poll of the Big East Conference's basketball coaches picked the 2001–2002 University of Pittsburgh basketball team to finish sixth in the West Division. There are seven teams in the division. In the most remarkable season any Pitt follower could remember, the Panthers shocked and surprised everybody but themselves. The Panthers won 29 games overall and lost only six. They won the Big East's West Division with a record of 13-3, the school's best-ever Big East mark. Pitt advanced to the championship game of the Big East Tournament for the second straight year. The Panthers then made it to the Sweet Sixteen of the NCAA Tournament for the first time in 28 years. Head coach Ben Howland and his players kept reminding everybody that they were legitimate. He pointed to the run his team made at the previous year's Big East Tournament, emphasizing how crucial and important that experience

would be for the nucleus of players coming back for the next season. Some critics pointed to a soft early-season schedule, but the Panthers kept on mowing down their opponents once the Big East schedule kicked in after January. It was a very good year.

From left to right are the following: (front row) Tony Tate, Julius Page, Brandin Knight, head coach Ben Howland, Carl Krauser, Yuri Demetris, Jaron Brown, and Chad Johnson; (back row) manager Dan Szramowski, athletic trainer Tony Salesi, director of operations Chris Carlson, associate head coach Jamie Dixon, assistant coach Ernie Ziegler, Ontario Lett, Donatas Zavackas, Mark McCarroll, Toree Morris, Chevon Troutman, Gino Federico, assistant coach Barry Rohrssen, video coordinator Kevin Roach, strength and conditioning coach Tim Beltz, manager John Janovsky, and manager Tariq Jamal-Francis.

127

In only his third season at the University of Pittsburgh, head coach Ben Howland directed the Panthers to their best season: 29 victories, more than any other season in school history. Howland received five national Coach of the Year honors in tribute to the job he did with the team. The Panthers finished the season ranked No. 7 in the USA Today/ESPN poll and No. 9 by the Associated Press. Shortly after the conclusion of the 2001–2002 season, he was rewarded with a contract extension through the 2008–2009 season. He plans on honoring it. "Trust me," he told a media gathering. "I'm going to be here a long, long time."